AGRICULTURAL BANKING

"Despite their significant role in making the country self-sufficient in its food needs, sadly farmers are still not in a position to make their own livelihood secure. With no easy access to farm credit timely raising their crop, no reliable system in place to insure the same against uncertainties and no stable market for their produce, farmers largely of small and marginal categories find farming a gamble. Often left with no option but to depend on private money lenders for crop loan at exorbitant interest rates which lands them into not easily recoverable debt trap, has resulted today in their rural livelihood base. The book, *Agricultural Banking: Getting the Perspective Right* authored by an eminent agricultural economist, traces chronologically how the public agricultural banking system evolved and is functioning since last 60 years. While highlighting the positive aspects of the farmer-oriented public lending system, the author does not fail in identifying its deficiencies as the reasons for the still thriving private money lending practice in rural India. Consideration of his views and suggestions for correcting the deficiencies in the public farm credit system, crop insurances and minimum support price would make them truly farmer-friendly."

E.A. Siddiq
Honorary Director
Institute of Biotechnology
Acharya N.G. Ranga Agricultural University
and
Distinguished Chair
Centre for DNA Fingerprinting and Diagnostics
Nampally, Hyderabad

Other books by the author with Konark Publishers

A Saint in the Board Room

Risk Management: The New Accelerator

AGRICULTURAL BANKING
GETTING THE PERSPECTIVE RIGHT

B. Yerram Raju

KONARK
Konark Publishers Pvt Ltd
New Delhi • Seattle

Konark Publishers Pvt. Ltd
206, First Floor,
Peacock Lane, Shahpur Jat,
New Delhi- 110 049
Phone: +91-11-41055065, 65254972
e-mail: india@konarkpublishers.com
website: www.konarkpublishers.com

Konark Publishers International
1507 Western Avenue, #605,
Seattle, WA 98101
Phone: (415) 409-9988
e-mail: us@konarkpublishers.com

Cataloging in Publication Data–DK
Courtesy: D.K. Agencies (P) Ltd. <docinfo@dkagencies.com>

Raju, B. Yerram, 1941-
Agricultural banking : getting the perspective right / B. Yerram Raju.
p. cm.
Includes bibliographical references (p.) and index.
ISBN 9789322008321

1. Banks and banking–India. 2. Rural credit–India. 3. Farm produce–India–Marketing. 4. Retail trade–India. I. Title.

DDC 332.10954 23

Editors: Rina Tripathi and Devika Dutt

Typeset by Saanvi Graphics, Noida, and printed and bound at Thomson Press (India) Ltd.

To all those farmers who laid their lives sunk
in private debt and in penury

Errata

Chapter, Page	Line	Correction
Preface, xi	One	After 'publishing' add: V. Jaganmohan
Introduction, xxvi	12	Read 'heaving' as 'heavy'
Introduction, xxiii	15	Read 'National Service Scheme' as 'National Sample Survey'
Introduction, xxxii	Column 3, Bottom cage (h)	Read 'Irrigation of facilities' as 'Irrigation facilities'
Chapter 1, 2	7	Read 'in to' as 'to'
Chapter 7, 62	17	Add the symbol for 'divided by' after present worth of benefits
Chapter 18, 163	3	Last word in the sentence: Read 'should' as 'share'

Contents

WATERSHED MANAGEMENT

AGRICULTURAL MARKETING AND ORGANIZED RETAIL TRADE

Foreword

This comprehensive book by Dr Yerram Raju on the history of Agricultural Banking and the role of institutions like NABARD in fostering food security and rural development is a timely one. Brain (that is, technology), brawn (that is, labour) and bank (that is, finance and other resources) are the three pillars for sustainable economic growth and agrarian and rural prosperity. Dr Yerram Raju, with his vast knowledge of the banking sector as well as the cooperative movement, has been able to capture the role of institutional credit in shaping the future of our agriculture.

The National Commission on Farmers (NCF), which I chaired, dealt with the issue of rural credit in an extensive manner. NCF stressed the need for making institutional credit available to farm families at 4 percent interest rate and I am glad that this has now become a reality. NCF also stressed the need for an integrated approach to credit and insurance on the one hand, and macro- and micro-finance on the other. There is a move now to institutionalize micro-credit programmes largely operated by Self-Help Groups (SHG) comprising mainly of women. The SHG movement has given women members the power and economies of scale in both production and marketing. The work of Nobel Laureate Muhammad Yunus in Bangladesh and Smt Ela Bhatt in India has shown how micro-credit can become a powerful ally in the struggle against poverty, unemployment and hunger. In this context, the stress by Dr Yerram Raju for a well planned rural credit policy is timely. Farmers' suicides are still largely continuing due to the lack of access to formal credit on the part of those who are already indebted.

Another weakness of our rural credit system, including the Kisan Credit Card programme of NABARD, is the inability of women farmers to have access to formal credit. This is because women farmers often do not have title to land which disqualifies them from getting the Kisan Credit Card or other sources of formal credit. Therefore, we need a careful review of our existing credit systems, particularly the emphasis placed now on financial inclusion. In particular, the direct transfer of benefits now being envisaged using the Aadhar platform which requires that everyone has a bank account.

Dr Yerram Raju has also dealt with other issues like Foreign Direct Investment in retail. I agree with him that rural India is crying for greater investment—whether foreign or national. There is a growing mismatch between production and post-harvest technologies. The production of fruits and vegetables now exceeds 250 million tonnes. Also, milk production is now over 130 million tonnes. All these perishable commodities require a well planned post-harvest processing, storage and marketing system like the one developed by the late Dr V. Kurien under Operation Flood's Phase I and II. However, it is necessary to ensure that FDI in retail is operated under a well planned ethical code. The bottom line should be the wellbeing and income security of farmers, and the satisfaction of consumers.

We owe a deep debt of gratitude to Dr Yerram Raju for this timely publication on agricultural banking. I hope it will be read and used widely by both professionals and policy makers.

M.S. Swaminathan
Founder Chairman
M.S. Swaminathan Research Foundation

Preface

When some of my good friends in publishing, and S. Subbaiah of the Reserve Bank of India (RBI) saw my articles on agriculture, rural development, poverty and governance, they suggested that I should select a few and republish them as a book because of their relevance to the present and future. I agreed to it, not realizing that the effort of scanning the scripts published over nearly 50 years would be hard work. Annually, on an average, 12 articles were published in various financial dailies like *The Economic Times*, *Financial Express*, *Business Standard*, *The Hindu Business Line* and *The Hindu* apart from writing a few chapters in books, a few seminar papers and a few articles in international journals.

The journey has been arduous, but has been made possible with the cooperation of a good researcher, Nori Usha, who painstakingly went through the material and provided the requisite inputs and data for updating the content where necessary. During my near three decades of experience as a practicing banker with the State Bank of India, I had the unique opportunity of learning about agriculture from the farmers through my interactions and working with them in the fields, with N. Rege, specialist in irrigation projects, B.S. Sathe, specialist in Animal Husbandry with the erstwhile Agriculture Refinance and Development Corporation. More than this, R.K. Talwar, the then Chairman, SBI, provided the soil test tool-kit and two books of the ICAR, *Hand Book of Agriculture* and *Hand Book of Animal Husbandry*, as extension support at the start of my career as an agent, in the Agricultural Development Branch, Visakhapatnam in 1971. He was certain that credit without an extension service would end in disaster, both for the bank and the farmer; a great visionary he was, the like of whom are few.

As the title of the book indicates, the aim is to get the perspective right and along with a historical view of agricultural banking in independent India. The content has been grouped into five distinct parts. The Introduction provides the historical perspective. The other parts are as below:

Part 1. Land Issues
Part 2. Farm and Rural Credit Issues
Part 3. Watershed Management
Part 4. Indian Agriculture in World Trade
Part 5. Agriculture Marketing and Organized Retail Trade.

I cannot forget a Telugu poem that I read when I was young, which when translated reads: "A village is uninhabitable if there is no moneylender, a doctor, a teacher, and a stream that never dries up." These four were institutionalized as the years went by. Moneylender, though this profession still exists, has been partly substituted with a Primary Agricultural Credit Cooperative Society, a branch of either a Regional Rural Bank or a commercial bank or in some places, all of them. Agriculture and credit are inextricably intertwined, for the farmer does not have cash when he direly needs it for investment or consumption, as it is locked up either in land or stock. Liquidity requirements drive him to the moneylender. The All India Debt and Investment Survey as on June 30, 2002[1] had shown that the share of moneylenders in the total dues of rural households increased from 17.5 percent in 1991 to 29.6 percent in 2002. The RBI in 2006 even toyed with the idea of regulating the moneylenders by institutionalizing them. A technical group was set up to review the legislation on moneylending in 2006–07 that suggested a model legislation in 2007. The public debate on the bill later had put it in cold storage due to its infeasibility.

Timely financing for every need of the farmer at the right time involves proper insights into the process, empathy with the farmer, full knowledge and understanding of his requirements for farm operations, consumption and investment. Despite more than 100 years of rural cooperatives, and over 40 years of commercial bank lending, such insights were not at par with the moneylenders residing in the village. Indigenous bankers, as they can safely be termed, proved their indispensability as they loan money on the basis of trust and not on security or guarantee from the borrower. The report of the Study Group of the Banking Commission on the indigenous bankers says it all: "The proper course would be for the Reserve Bank to exercise direct influence over the business of indigenous bankers through the medium of commercial banks…Because they remain outside the rigid cast-iron framework of rules and regulations and they are able to operate with a certain degree of flexibility, which is what attracts the small borrower."

The distinction between the moneylender, and those lending from within the family—a doctor, a lawyer or other relatives—is variation in interest and not so much in terms of accessing or acquiring the borrowers' assets when the latter defaults for long spells. The hanging rope descends on the borrower's neck not with immediate default but after consecutive failures; many a time, such default is extended beyond a generation. Such long waits are untenable in institutional credit. Secondly, such extended credits have their dark shadow of high interest rates, called as usurious. The moneylenders do exercise coercive measures that have received acceptance in society but never by law. Mostly, land owned by the farmer and his family is the basis for lending.

The institutions that stepped in could only reduce the monopoly. Nationalization of banks was the point of inflexion. Between 1969 and 1990, commercial banks in general, the newborn regional rural banks and nationalized banks in particular, through the agriculture-intensive branches, did achieve spectacular results. At a time when institutions were on the verge of replacing the moneylenders in 1990, the share of moneylenders in farm credit came down to approximately 40 percent. This community, most of whom are legislators and parliamentarians, hatched a plan to kill the institutional credit through waiver of loans. Though the quantum of the waiver was Rs 10,000 crore, and was to be extended to mostly small and marginal farmers, due to several vested interests, the waiver landed up becoming a bonanza for the large farmers who were not the targeted beneficiaries. The process created a precedence for such waivers and the state governments started waiving interest on loans in the name of helping farmers in distress, due to crop or asset losses, periodically; the Rs 72,000 crore waiver of 2008 finally killed institutional credit. Thereafter, it was only targets for crop loans that were mercifully shown as achieved; but the number of farmers' suicides due to excessive debt increased in states like Andhra Pradesh, Maharashtra, Punjab and Karnataka. All that a farmer needed was assured credit at softer interest rates and standard operating procedures (SOPS) in distress caused by natural calamities, and the confidence that the next crop and family would not starve for want of the required finance. This assurance rests still with the moneylender.

A word about the moneylending legislation in all 28 states would be in order.

This has been ably summarized in the Report of the Technical Group (op.cit) 2008 as follows:

1. Requirement of registration/license for carrying on the business of moneylending within a state/a portion of the state duties of the moneylenders with respect to maintaining and providing a statement of accounts to debtors.
2. Penalties for carrying on business without license and for intimidating the debtors or interfering with their day-to-day activities, including the cognizability of such offences.
3. Maximum interest rates that can be charged.
4. Matters that the courts are required/empowered to decide in suits filed by moneylenders.
5. Applicability to companies engaged in the moneylending business. However, some states in exercise of their general exemption powers, granted exemptions to companies from the applicability of the legislation.
6. Exemption to loans from a trader to another trader, loans by banks, cooperative societies, financial institutions, etc.

Land owned by the farmer has been subject to subdivision and fragmentation for generations. The records relating to these are expected to be carried out by the revenue authorities—the mutations—starting from the village revenue officers (known as *Patwaris* in some parts and *Karanams* in some other parts of the state). This institution had been abolished during the regime of N.T. Rama Rao, and thereafter, the *zamabandis* or verification of land records every year by the Joint Collectors of the districts, was also abolished. There were a number of recommendations by various committees for computerization of land records and issue of *pattadar* passbooks as safe instruments of security in the hands of the lenders. Issues relating to these aspects have been dealt with in a few articles from time to time that figure in Part I of this book.

The major reforms introduced in the banking sector since 1969 are nationalization of major banks and liberalization of the sector. Based on size of deposits, 14 private banks in 1969 and 6 private banks in 1980 were nationalized. The important reasons for nationalization of banks were: (a) increasing bank network, especially in rural and semi-urban areas; (b) larger mobilization of resources and; (c) redirection of credit flows, especially to priority sector and weaker sections.[2] In order to achieve the above objectives, many measures were taken, which include (a) branch licensing polices linked to rural branch expansion; (b) fixing high percentage lending to priority sector; (c) maintaining 60 percent Credit Deposit (CD) ratio with respect to rural areas; (d) financing government deficit by fixing higher Statutory Liquidity Ratio (SLR); (e) fixing high Cash Reserve Ratio (CRR); (f) fixing lending targets for anti-poverty programmes; (g) cross subsidisation from large to small borrowers and also to priority sectors from other sectors; (h) preparation of district credit plans; (g) preparation of annual credit plan for each bank, and; (h) restrictions on the entry of new banks. By and large, the objectives of nationalization were met through these measures.

These measures, however, came in the way of profitability and efficiency. The reasons for decline in the efficiency/profits were (a) high Cash Reserve Ratio (CRR) and Statutory Liquidity Ratio (SLR); (b) low yield rates on government bonds; (c) low quality of credit resulting in high Non-Performing Asset (NPA); (d) cross subsidization with administered interest rates; (e) lack of competition among the banks and; (f) laxity in supervision. As a result of the recommendations of the Committee on Financial Sector Reforms (Narasimham Committee-1, Government of India, New Delhi), post-liberalization reforms lead to closing un-remunerative rural branches, restructuring the Regional Rural Banks that truncated from 196 to 82, and gradual decline of agricultural credit, particularly investment credit for agriculture. This situation was sought to be remedied through redefining priority sector and allocation of targets to commercial banks. The impact has been dealt with in a number of articles from time to time by me. They have all been grouped in the second part of the book: Farm and Rural Credit Policies. Although references to the functioning of Regional Rural Banks and Farmers' Service Societies have been made in a few articles, I have not done a detailed review of the restructuring of these two sets of institutions in my published articles, and therefore, the reader may find a gap in this area.

Part 3 deals with waste land development as a bankable proposition; its evolution, the support given by the NABARD, and a few aspects that the evaluation studies brought out in lending for these schemes, in the context of nearly 60 percent of land remaining as rain fed.

Part 4 deals with impact of the World Trade Organization (WTO) on Indian agriculture. The role of agriculture in Indian exports has been dealt with in a few articles.

Part 5 deals with the issues relating to agricultural marketing, organized retailing and the interrelationship of a farmer's prosperity with the marketing aspects.

The last chapter deals with the way forward, putting in a nutshell several strategies that were discussed in various articles that have relevance today.

Since these articles were written at different points of time, the data would be naturally relevant to the time of writing the article. Updating the data in such articles would diminish the historical perspective. Wherever such updating of facts does not affect the perspective, it has been attempted. The reader may also feel burdened in the process with some repetition. I request patience in this regard. Editing such parts might have led to discontinuity in the thought process and approach to these articles. However, grouping of articles has been done with some modifications wherever possible to provide convenience, continuity and comfort to the reader.

Notes

1. B. Yerram Raju, 2005, NSS 59th Round, December.
2. Rangarajan, 1989.

Introduction

'Most of the world's poor people earn their living from agriculture, so if we knew the economics of agriculture, we would know much of the economics of being poor.'

—Theodore W. Schultz

Vision for Agricultural Development

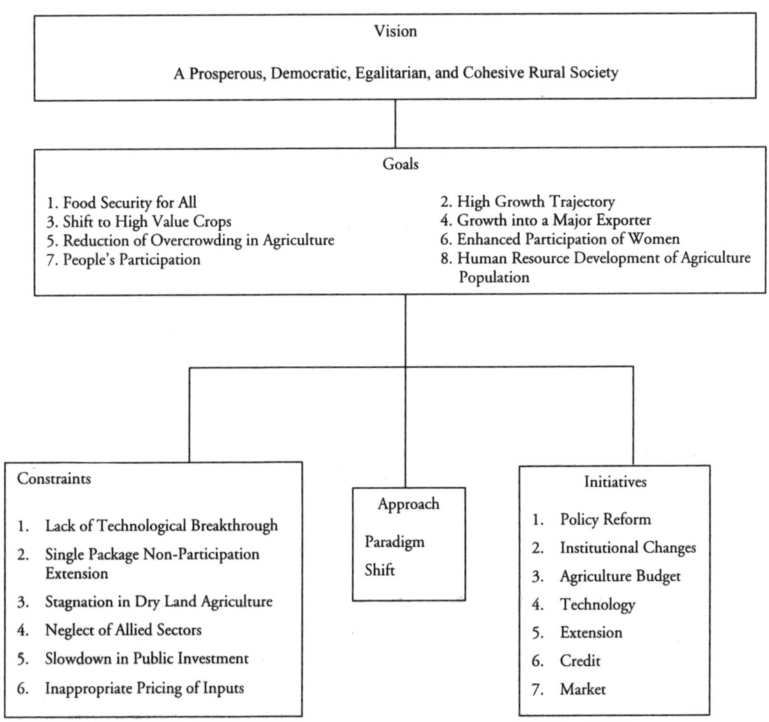

Structure and Structural Transformation of Indian Agriculture

Global economic changes in the last few decades have exposed every nation to the highly precarious economic environment, thus creating challenges especially for an agrarian economy. India is an agrarian economy; agriculture supports nearly 70 percent of the population and provides food security. However, there was a sharp fall in its share in the country's Gross Domestic Product (GDP), from 30 percent in 1990–91 to 14.5 percent in 2011–12. A rapid growth in the services sector boosted the share of services in the GDP, surpassing that of the agricultural sector. It is interesting to note that despite the fall in agriculture's share in the country's total output, even now 52 percent of the workforce is dependent on agriculture.[1]

Sectoral Composition of GDP

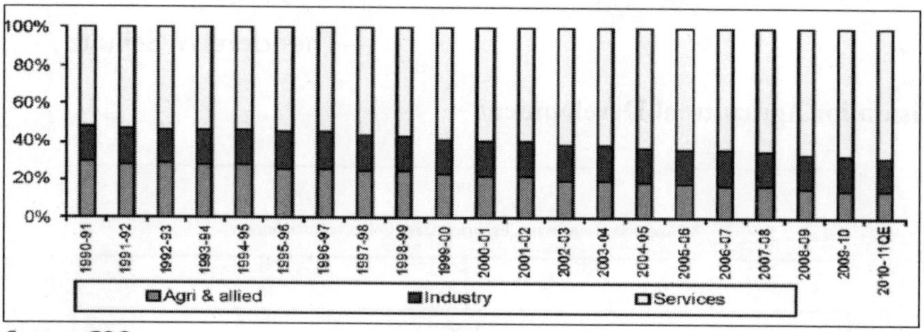

Source: CSO.

Another weakness of the sector is the problem of diminishing operational land holding size. The average size of operational holdings has diminished progressively from 2.28 ha in 1970–71 to 1.55 ha in 1990–91 to 1.23 ha in 2005–06. As per Agriculture Census 2005–06, the proportion of marginal holdings (area less than 1 ha) has increased from 61.6 percent in 1995–96 to 64.8 percent in 2005–06. This is followed by about 18 percent small holdings (1–2 ha), about 16 percent medium holdings (more than 2 to less than 10 ha) and less than 1 percent large holdings (10 ha and above).

Growth Performance of Agriculture: Overall Growth

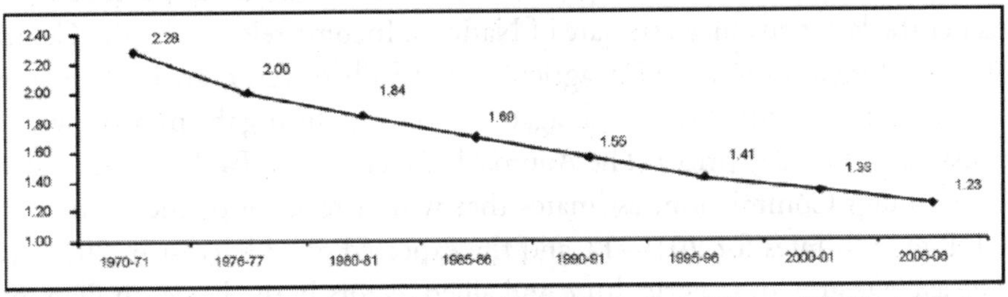

Source: Department of Agriculture and Cooperation, Agricultural Census Division, Ministry of Agriculture.

Growth Rates: GDP (Overall) and GDP (Agriculture and Allied Sectors)

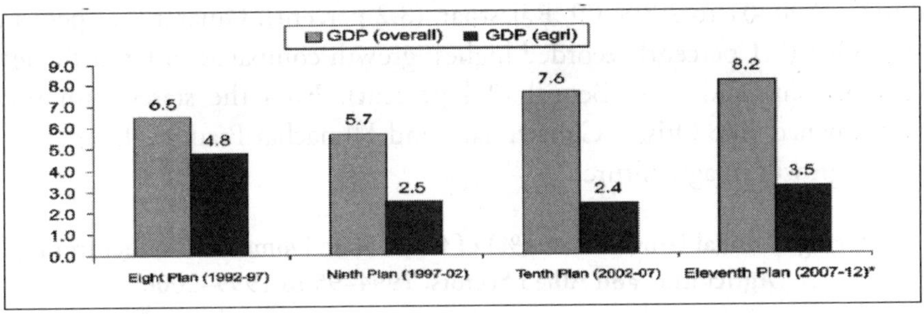

Source: CSO.
*Note: *Figure for the Eleventh Plan show growth rates for the first four years of the Plan.*

The growth rates would give a clearer picture about the status of the sector. It is quite evident that the agriculture sector has been performing badly since the Ninth Plan period. While the agriculture growth rate was 4.8 percent during the Eighth Plan period (1992–97), the subsequent plan periods (1997–2002 and 2002–07) witnessed a steep fall in the growth rates, thus registering 2.5 percent and 2.4 percent respectively. In contrast, the Indian economy has shown a progressive growth rate of 7.6 percent during the Tenth Plan period.

Attempts to reverse the deceleration of agricultural growth since the Ninth Plan by the Government of India helped the nation achieve some success in the food grain production. The food grain production touched a new peak of 250.42 million tonnes in 2011–12.

Agricultural GDP growth has accelerated to an average of 3.9 percent during 2005–06 to 2010–11, partly because of initiatives taken since 2004. As per the latest advance estimate of National Income released by the Central Statistics Organization (CSO), agriculture and allied sectors are likely to grow at 2.5 percent during 2011–12 as against 7 percent during the previous year at constant (2004–05) prices. The Approach Paper for the Twelfth Plan drafted by Planning Commission, estimates that with a revision of the farm sector GDP growth rates for 2010–11 and the expected good harvest in 2011–12. The average growth in agriculture and allied sectors in the Eleventh Plan may be higher, at 3.3–3.5 percent per year against a target of 4 percent.

Regional Variations in Growth

At the regional level, the growth performance of agriculture shows that during 2000–01 to 2008–09, Rajasthan (8.2 percent), Gujarat (7.7 percent) and Bihar (7.1 percent) recorded highest growth compared to Uttar Pradesh (2.3 percent) and West Bengal (2.4 percent). Even the states with poor performance, like Orissa, Chhattisgarh and Himachal Pradesh, have shown strong growth in agriculture.

Average Annual Growth Rate (%) of Gross State Domestic Product from Agriculture and Allied Sectors, 1994–95 to 1999–2000

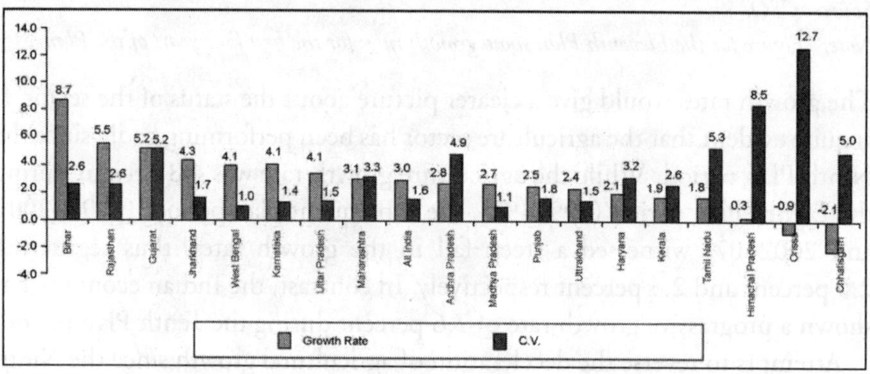

Average Annual Growth Rate (%) of Gross State Domestic Product from Agriculture and Allied Sectors, 2000–01 to 2008–09

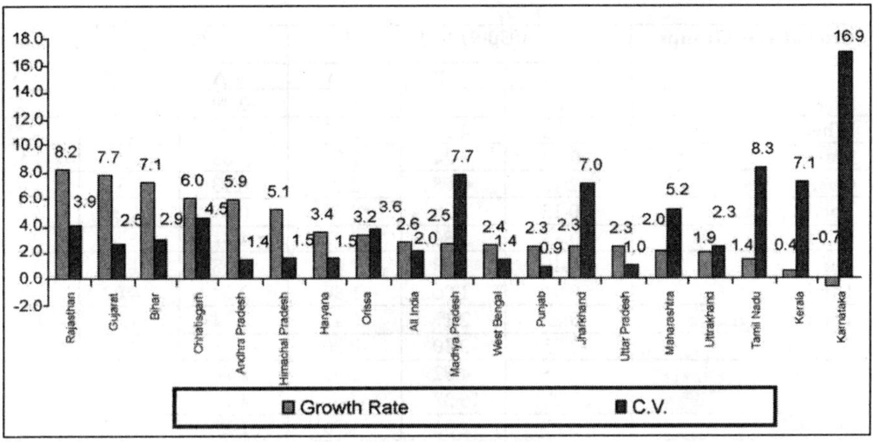

Source: Economic Survey, Government of India, Hand Book of Indian Statistics, RBI, various years.

Crop-Specific Growth

During 2010–11, food grains production was 244.78 million tonnes, comprising of 121.14 million tonnes during Kharif season and 123.64 million tonnes during the Rabi season. Of the total food grains production, production of cereals was 226.54 million tonnes and pulses 18.24 million tonnes. Production of rice was estimated at 102.75 million tonnes, wheat 88.31 million tonnes, coarse cereals 42.08 million tonnes and pulses 17.28 million tonnes. Oil seeds production during 2011–12 is estimated at 30.53 million tonnes, sugarcane production is estimated at 347.87 million tonnes and cotton production is estimated at 34.09 million bales (of 170 kg each). Jute production has been estimated at 10.95 million bales (of 180 kg each). Despite inconsistent climatic factors in some parts of the country, there has been a record production, surpassing the targeted production of 245 million tonnes of food grains by more than 5 million tonnes during 2011–12.

All India Average Annual Growth Rates of Area, Production and Yield of Principal Crops (%)

Crops/Crop Groups	1990-91 to 1999-2000			2000-01 to 2010-11		
	A	P	Y	A	P	Y
Rice	0.70	2.09	1.36	-0.39	1.32	1.47
Wheat	1.62	4.52	2.87	0.57	1.39	0.73
Maize	0.85	2.24	1.37	2.68	7.12	4.13
Coarse Cereals	-2.42	-0.08	2.03	-0.13	5.0	4.64
Total Cereals	-0.12	2.29	2.38	-0.09	1.82	1.69
Gram	0.88	3.86	2.97	4.31	6.39	1.19
Tur	-0.45	1.89	2.03	2.58	1.89	-0.65
Total Pulses	-0.91	1.06	1.82	2.30	4.02	1.21
Total Foodgrains	-0.27	2.19	2.43	0.34	1.95	1.37
Groundnut	-2.25	-2.40	-0.30	-1.08	13.13	12.76
R & M	2.28	4.82	2.96	2.76	6.26	2.72
Soyabean	11.01	16.37	4.67	4.15	8.31	4.17
Oilseeds	0.75	2.53	1.76	1.27	7.00	5.18
Sugarcane	2.25	3.16	0.91	1.95	2.12	0.03
Cotton	1.42	0.93	-0.54	2.66	12.12	9.15

Source: Directorate of Economics & Statistics, Ministry of Agriculture.
Note: A: Area, P: Production, Y: Yield.

All the major coarse cereals display a negative growth in area during both the periods, except for maize which recorded an annual growth rate of 2.68 percent in 2000–01 to 2010–11. The production of maize has also increased by 7.12 percent in the latter period. In pulses, gram recorded a growth of 6.39 percent in production during the same period, driven by expansion in the area under cultivation. Soybean has recorded a high rate of growth in production in both the periods, driven primarily by expansion in area under cultivation. In fact, oil seeds as a group has shown some significant changes in the two decades; the production growth rate has more than doubled in the decade of 2000s, compared to the previous decade, driven both by productivity gains (for example groundnut and soybean) as well as by area gains. The average annual growth rates of production and productivity of groundnut during 2000–01 to 2010–11 are abnormally high due to high fluctuations in the production and productivity during the years 2002–03, 2006–07 and 2007–08. The trend of growth rates in the production and productivity of groundnut during 2000–01 to 2010–11 works out to 1.66 percent and 2.63 percent respectively. Fruits and vegetables have shown a higher growth in production and area in 2000–01 to 2010–11 as compared to 1990–91 to 1999–2000.

The biggest increase in the growth rates of yields in the two periods however, is in groundnut and cotton. Cotton has experienced significant changes with the introduction of *Bacillus thuringiensis* (Bt) cotton in 2002. By 2011–12, almost 90 percent of cotton area was covered under Bt cotton, production has more than doubled (compared to 2002–03), yields have gone up by almost 70 percent, and an export potential for more than Rs 10,000 crore worth of raw cotton per year has been created. Many more such revolutions to accelerate agricultural growth are needed.

The post-World Trade Organization (WTO) economic environment has a major impact on the Indian agricultural sector in terms of both challenges and opportunities. Despite high levels of production, there are several structural weaknesses that need to be addressed to make our agriculture more competitive, domestically and globally. Continued priority will have to be given to the primary concern of ensuring domestic food and nutritional security. According to National Service Scheme (NSS) estimates, the number of people below the minimum nutritional requirement of 2400 Kcal per day constitutes 42 percent of the rural population and 48.8 percent of the urban population[2]. The policy focus seems to be shifting to export-oriented agriculture and a demand-driven production system. Our share in world trade in agricultural commodities is barely 1 percent and our share in world agricultural production is around 12 percent. In the emerging economic environment, Indian agriculture will be more and more closely inter-linked with global markets. This process picked up momentum in the year 2005 when the WTO-stipulated commitments in the Agreement on Agriculture were fully operationalized. This will mean reduction in domestic support (in the form of producer subsidies), greater market access and removal of export subsidies. These WTO provisions will have a likely impact on the livelihoods of 200 million farmers and agricultural workers throughout the country.

Indian agriculture has increasingly been opened up to global agriculture with agricultural exports and imports as a percentage of agricultural GDP rising from 4.9 percent in 1990–91 to 12.7 percent in 2010–11. This is still low as compared to the share of India's total exports and imports as a percentage of India's GDP at 55.7 percent. India is a net exporter of agricultural commodities with agricultural exports constituting 11 percent of India's total exports. However, the share of agricultural exports in India's overall exports has been declining from 18.5 percent in 1990–91 to 10.5 percent in 2010–11.

Trends in Trade of Agricultural Commodities

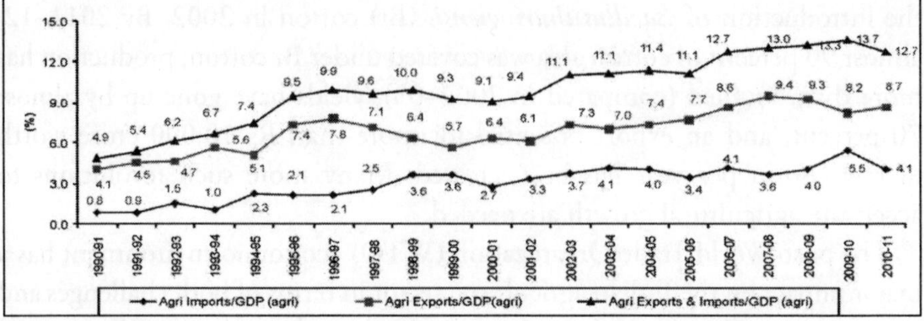

Source: Compiled from the Annual Reports of the Union Ministry of Commerce and Industry, Government of India.

These trends signal the need for greater integration of local markets with external markets. India's competitiveness relies on infrastructure development and better institutional mechanism, which enables a deeper integration of domestic markets across global markets.

Indian Agriculture in World Trade

India is among the 15 leading exporters of agricultural products in the world. India's agricultural exports amounted to US$ 17 billion with a share of 1.4 percent of world trade in agriculture in the year 2009. On the other hand, India's agricultural imports amounted to US$ 14 billion with a share of 1.2 percent of world trade in agriculture.[3]

Agricultural exports increased from Rs 89,341.50 crore in 2009–10 to Rs 1,20,185.95 crore during 2010–11, registering a growth of about 34.52 percent. Increase in value of agricultural exports during 2010–11 was primarily on account of higher exports of sugar, molasses, cotton, guar gum meal, spices, niger seed, groundnut, maize, coffee, oil meal, castor oil, tea and jute, compared to the corresponding period of the previous year. However, the share of agricultural exports in total exports decreased slightly from 10.57 percent in 2009–10 to 10.47 percent in 2010–11.

Agricultural imports recorded an overall decrease from Rs 59,528.33 crore in 2009–10 to Rs 56,196.20 crore in 2010–11, registering a decline of 5.6 percent over the corresponding previous period. Decrease in the value of agricultural imports during this period was primarily due to lower imports of pulses, sugar and cotton. The share of agricultural imports in total imports also decreased from 4.37 percent in 2009–10 to 3.50 percent in 2010–11. Over the years, India has experienced surplus in its agriculture trade. This increased trade, particularly from Rs 29,813.17 crore in 2009–10 to Rs 63,989.75 crore in 2010–11 is the result of higher exports of cotton, sugar and oil meal products.

India's Major Agricultural Exports

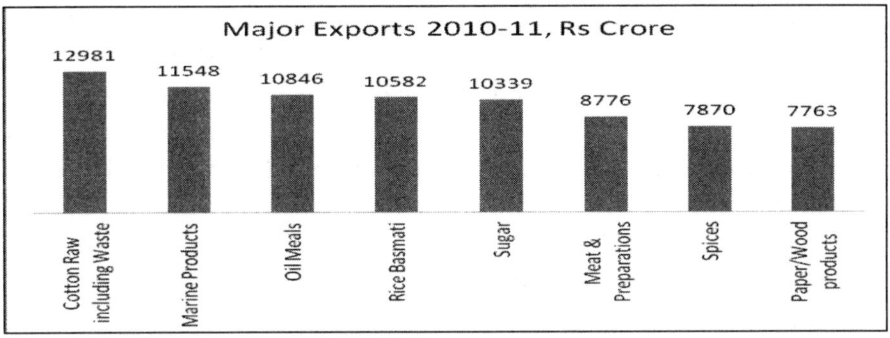

India's Major Agricultural Imports

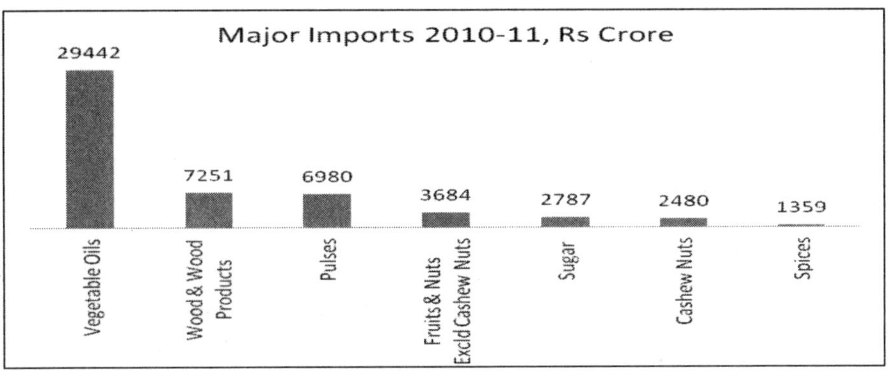

Further, how the Indian farmer responds to the trade and agricultural policy changes will depend on his ability to access information, respond quickly to market signals and manage risk efficiently. Much will depend on the type of strategies that are adopted for increasing the capabilities of farmers to exploit the advantages of open markets. Policy interventions that are crop-specific, region-specific and ensure appropriate support from the stage of crop production to marketing/export, are needed. The National Agricultural Policy (2000) has set out a comprehensive framework, which emphasizes sustainable land and water resource management through ecologically-sound agricultural practices, efficient input-use, infrastructure development and appropriate pre- and post-harvest technologies. Agricultural growth is targeted at 4 percent.

Policies designed to influence decision-making of millions of individual farmers across the country must take note of the fact that about 75 percent of farmers are in the small and marginal category, operating farms of less than 2 hectares. The situation of these farmers is extremely vulnerable. Consider a factory worker—wearing a uniform, getting an annual bonus, securing health protection either through Employees' State Insurance (ESI) or otherwise, working in the comfort of a mostly indoor, organized environment. Compare that with the farmer's working environment—in the open, under the hot sun or in heaving rain, managing all inputs for production himself, unsure of produce at the end of his toil, therefore, facing uncertain income. Can the assurance of a rational Minimum Support Price (MSP) be removed when 75 percent of farmers fall into this category?

Our farmers face severe problems in accessing credit, getting remunerative prices and marketing their produce. About two-thirds of India's cropped area–producing coarse cereals, pulses, oil seeds, cotton and rice—is rain-fed, making the farmers in these areas highly vulnerable to drought and resource-constraints. Productivity for major crops in India is low, and in most cases, productivity is only half of the international average for that particular commodity. Availability of certified seeds is limited; spurious seeds and pesticides have become a serious problem. Extension services reach only 25–30 percent of farmers in the country. Better information sharing between providers and users of technology can improve institutional quality. This requires liberalization of agricultural research and extension services to strengthen existing institutions. The World Development Report (2002) has summarized the functions of Extension Services as follows: "To inform farmers of new products and techniques, and to gather and transfer information from farmers to other participants. This includes collecting feedback on farmer needs as input for research priorities, and learning techniques from one farmer and sharing them with others, for example, irrigation techniques."[4] The role of Non-governmental Organizations (NGOs) in extension, like Society for Research and Initiatives for Sustainable Technologies and Institutions (SRISTI) in Gujarat had helped a great deal in providing dependable extension services on time, and at minimum cost. Declining public investment, slow pace of irrigation development, weak infrastructure and ineffective price policy for major crops are some of the major constraints in the way of restructuring the agricultural sector.

Against this backdrop, what are the issues relevant to the farmer in the post-WTO scenario, and which need increased awareness so that effective strategies can be formulated?

Issues

Raising competitiveness by reducing costs and increasing quality levels is crucial for any future strategy to develop the agricultural sector. Farmers need to know the problems and solutions related to the specific crop grown by them.

1. Increasing productivity for major crops and the most effective ways of achieving this through better use of inputs, improved crop practices—Integrated Pest Management (IPM) and Integrated Nutrient Management (INM)—within a sustainable framework of resource-management.
2. Emphasis on sustainable agricultural development through conservation of bio-diversity and the existing natural resource base/eco-systems.
3. Diversification of agriculture—combination of crop-livestock activities along with other options to shift farmers away from mono-crop agriculture.
4. Raising cropping intensity through multi-cropping and inter-cropping practices.
5. Flexibility in crop patterns to respond to market signals and take advantage of emerging opportunities. For this, awareness of changes in consumption patterns for agricultural commodities in domestic and foreign markets is needed.
6. Awareness of price structures for both inputs and outputs.

Several innovative strategies for effective dissemination of market information are now being explored. For example, the Government of Andhra Pradesh makes prices available of produce in different regional markets on a website that is updated daily.

Access to credit is the main problem faced by farmers. One study of the rural environment states "Few banks would even consider making agricultural loans, and those who did, charge extremely high interest rates. Rural credit was fertile ground for loan sharks, and year after year, farmers turned over their crops to help pay exorbitant interest charges on loans made to keep their farms operating. Should a crop fail, the chances of a farmer extricating himself and his family from a loan shark's clutches was virtually non–existent."[5] Asymmetry in information enhances the risk of the lender and, therefore, information and enforcement mechanisms, particularly in regard to the titles the farmers hold, would enhance opportunities for accessing credit markets.

For export crops, farmers should have thorough knowledge of sanitary and phytosanitary norms and standards as implemented by importing countries. Under the Agreement on Sanitary and Phytosanitary Standards (SPS), every country has the freedom to choose the appropriate level of protection.

Farmers need to be made fully aware of the possibilities of bio-technological interventions, the potential benefits of transgenic crops and those with drought-resistant and pest-resistant properties. Awareness of bio-safety risks is also needed.

Knowledge base has to be developed for farmers' needs and priorities at every stage of activity, from cultivation to marketing/export. The regulations relating to product standards, protection of environment, and health and safety of citizens of the importing country are extremely important. It is not as though these standards are immune from market distorting influences. The developed nations seem to want free trade but it is not necessarily a fair trade. For example, the Met Matrices for fruits, vegetables, flowers, plants, fish and aquaculture, demonstrate the unsuitability of all standards under all circumstances.

Value addition in the production chain must be an area of special focus in the present context. There are several by-products for most agricultural commodities, which can be effectively developed through setting up agro-based and agro-processing industries that will not only raise rural incomes and employment but also create useful link between the agricultural and industrial sectors. Such a strategy requires farmer-managed organizations.

Role of Farmers' Associations

There is an urgent need for collaboration and co-operation among farmers/ farmers' groups to get the best advantage from inputs (seeds, water, fertilizers, pesticides, etc). Such co-operation presently exists under a political banner, but not under the banner of 'Production.'

District Farmers' Associations need to function without political affiliation for all aspects of agricultural production to assist farmers.

Farmers should set up Vigilance Councils at village/*mandal* levels to enforce regulation of laws impacting their future.

Unity among farmers generally comes to the fore in times of natural calamities, widespread pest attacks, holocausts, etc. The state has to re-engineer the insurance mechanisms for timely rejuvenation and risk reduction, deriving advantage from such unity.

If the District Farmers' Associations federate into a company, the federal body can directly plan and execute exports and seek infrastructure support. It has been the experience in the agricultural sector that capital formation in the public sector, triggered private capital formation as a sustainable measure, and this would need to be continued. Finally, "farmers operate in markets that suffer from problems of information, inadequate competition, and weak enforcement of contracts. Building institutions that reduce transaction costs to farmers, therefore, can greatly improve the way agricultural markets operate."[6]

Linking farmers to markets is a key focus area. E-commerce will be of great help in this area.

Specific problems in marketing include grading, standardization, storage and transport. Efforts in the public or private sectors to build specific institutions that ease information costs, such as grades and standards or market information systems, can help increase agricultural production. Setting up cold storage facilities and key infrastructure facilities, including transportation facilities to strengthen the supply chain for agricultural produce, holds the key to farmer prosperity.

District Farmers' Associations should act as hubs for sharing resources/technologies/marketing information. Role of Krishi Vigyan Kendras needs to be strengthened.

Role of the state in providing credit, infrastructure, free movement of agricultural produce (intra-state and inter-state), up-dating and consolidation of land records, development of a lease market for land (to promote contract farming and agri-business) becomes extremely important. Crop Insurance Schemes should be restructured and implemented effectively.

Information dissemination through a wide range of channels (print, electronic, etc) is another important area where both the state and the Farmers' Associations have a crucial role to play.

In fact, it is not the WTO Agreement or the lack of it that is important; it is proper policy formulation for the agricultural sector and creating enabling mechanisms for the farmers to play their role effectively without compromising their interests, that are important. The most important point to be noted is that it would no longer be possible to insulate ourselves from global impacts, and we should modify our processes, systems and policies to meet the emerging challenges.

The Seattle riots, the street shows in Geneva at the G8 meet, the tensions arising from the change in trade perspectives of Europe and the US—the two major trading blocs—are all pointers to the Doha WTO meet being not-so-smooth. The US got assurances from China, whose entry is almost certain, for its own trade protection. When a developed country threatened with a cut in its market share has taken pains to safeguard its market, should not India prepare well?

First, India has to equip the primary and secondary sectors to meet the standards of international markets. How does the Indian farmer cope with diverse demands? The last two decades witnessed inefficient and excessive use of chemical fertilizers and insecticides that has raised issues of food safety. While the GDP contribution of agriculture declined from 51 percent in 1954 to 24.8 percent in 1999–2000, the number of people dependent on agriculture has not. Productivity of any and every crop is either half or less than half of the global average.

It is a fact that all developed countries have been heavily subsidizing their agriculture and small and medium enterprises (SMEs) because the contribution of these sectors to their GDP is low. In five decades of misdirected subsidies and none-to-blame weak administrative machinery dispensing them, with barely 3 percent of gross revenue surpluses remaining for developmental expenditure, India does not have the money to keep subsidy coming. It is this appalling situation that is unnerving the Indian farmer.

States rich and abundant in natural resources—Bihar, Madhya Pradesh, eastern Uttar Pradesh, Assam, Meghalaya, Orissa, and so on—are excluded from development interventions at the farmer level because of political uncertainty, and problems on the ground. These states need to be brought into the production mainstream, to tap the ready export market.

Rice, wheat, maize, jowar, ragi and bajra, can all have related agro-based industries, for both off-season and round-the-year employment. But these would require utilization of appropriate post-harvest technologies. At the micro level, installation of technologies and provision of infrastructure facilities, such as power at uniform voltage, packaging, and so on, become critical. At the macro level, branding and co-branding of products that are to sell both in the domestic and export markets will become extremely important.

The country can develop competence in pisciculture/aquaculture. However, there are standards for many of these sectors. Therefore, it is important to set up testing laboratories at the landing sites and develop a vigilance mechanism to prevent imports of set-up standard products. At the same time, it should be possible to export large quantities. This would call for investment in specific packaging, safe and appropriate containers, and good local transport facilities with cold storage vans.

The sudden surpluses of grain have not found an outlet despite all the incentives offered to the states. Farmers' associations that are at a nascent stage of development, therefore, assume the role of export-traders.

Recently, a farmer association leader, addressing the former Chairman of the WTO Task Force, Sharad Joshi, raised an important question: "The Fifth Pay Commission doled out Rs 80,000 crore in a cash-starved economy to organized labour. What did the nation get in return? If a portion of it were to be given to the farm sector through properly directed subsidies, as in the developed nations, the Indian farmer would have given back in value-addition at least 40–50 percent of what they got."

The capital market is caught up in scams. Banks are awash with non-performing assets. The tax administration is inefficient. Neither the equity nor the debt market is immediately capable of delivering results. The liberalization of the financial sector did not make them efficient. Productive capital resources went in to recapitalizing bankrupt outfits. Financial institutions and banks are not dispensing credit where it is most needed, but in areas of convenience. The nation has to find resources to make the primary sector competitive in such a depressing scenario.

India has a minuscule 1.1 percent share of world exports. It faces the threat of imports, especially post-WTO. The Indian farmer has the ability to meet the emerging needs of the economy, provided he is given the wherewithal and infrastructure support.

As things stand, the farmer is unsure of his future. If he increases his production and productivity through higher resource-use efficiency, where will he store his surpluses until a market is found? When and how will he achieve the value-addition required by the external market? The WTO offers tremendous opportunities but India has to catch up on many fronts to take advantage of these.

Problem–Solution Matrix (From the Farmer's Point of View)

	Problem	Solution	
High	a) Ever rising costs of cultivation b) Inadequate capital (tools and machineries) c) Uninterrupted power supply d) Lack of timely credit e) Lack of irrigation facilities and high dependence on rainfall f) Inadequate Supply of quality seeds (quantity and timeliness) g) Inadequate marketing support h) Improper and inadequate technology i) High debts j) Delay in soil analysis/ recommendations	a) Free power tariff/writing off past dues b) Supply of farm inputs c) Integrated crop management i) Polam badi ii) SRI cultivation iii) Supply of inputs iv) Seed village programme/seed distribution v) Training of farmers vi) Vermi compost d) Credit delivery/credit intensification	High
Low	a) Lack of social groups/farmers clubs for awareness creation and boosting self confidence among the farmers for their empowerment b) Inadequate extension staff c) Unsatisfactory crop insurance d) No voice of farmers on marketing Boards e) Crop diversification f) Combination of allied and non-farm activities with agriculture towards sustainability	a) Restructuring of RMGs b) Very slow increase in extension staff c) Pilot crop insurance on village basis d) Enactment of model bill on market committee e) Slow crop diversification f) Agriculture technology mission g) WTO preparedness/ WTO cell/ICT h) Irrigation of facilities through major and medium irrigation brief i) Soil testing-implementing recommendations	Low

Known Problems

Not confronted

Academicians, department of agriculture, scientists, and high-level committees recognized that problems exist in a few areas and the solutions have also been offered. But, somehow on the field, no initiative is noted on the part of the department to implement those solutions.

Known Problems		To Be Confronted	
Gap Analysis	a) Non-farm activities related to crop activity as a package to the potential farmers/farmers' groups. b) Area wise studies on gap in yield of important crops to move in tandem with other progressive states c) Separation of regulatory functions from the facilitator–provider of services (Agricultural Department)	a) Appropriate integration of farming systems to regenerate natural resources b) Arrangement to market produce by local institutions like RMGs/SHGs/ cooperative societies. c) Revival and, formation of new Farmers Club by involving banks/NABARD and RMGs for empowering farmers. d) Housing of the major departments connected with agriculture and rural development in the same complex/ locality for administrative convenience and better coordination at the district/block/*mandal* level and also to offer quick services to the farming community e) Appropriate combination of allied activities with agriculture at the farmer level	Gap Analysis

Notes

1. B. Yerram Raju, NSS 66th Round.
2. B. Yerram Raju, 1993-94, NSS 50th Round.
3. B. Yerram Raju, 1993-94, International trade statistics.
4. B. Yerram Raju, 2002, World Development Report, p. 45
5. B. Yerram Raju, 2002, World Development Report, p. 39
6. B. Yerram Raju, World Development Report, p. 31.

CHAPTER 1

Reviving Agricultural Non-Farm Employment and Cooperatives

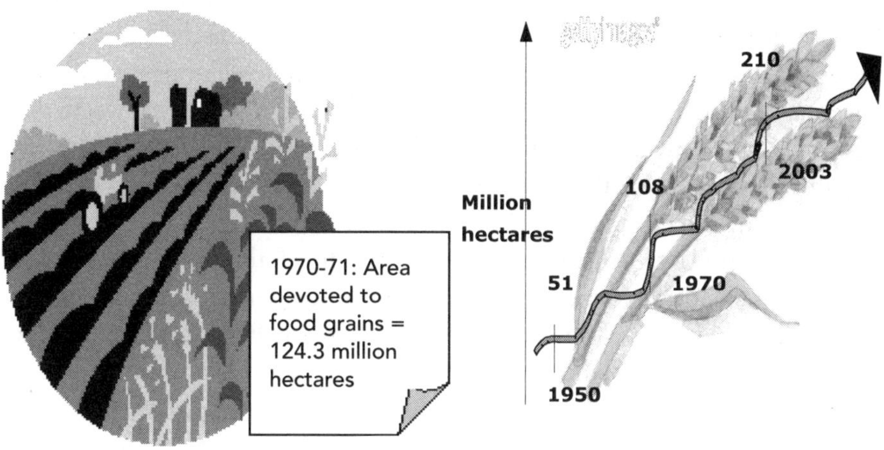

Figure 1.1: Food Production (mt)

The growth of the Indian economy continues to depend on the sustainable growth rate of the agricultural sector, as 62 percent of the population continues to depend on it. Promotion of growth and eradication of poverty continue to be the objectives of India's economic policy ever since planned economic development was launched in this country. It is a moot question whether and to what extent the poor have benefited in the process. What needs to be recognized however, is that the agrarian economy moved away from famines to increased production and productivity, and higher buffer stocks of grains that prompted the Supreme Court to call for distribution of grains for free to the starving poor. During the last three decades or the six Five-Year Plan periods, growth rates of agriculture largely depending on favourable monsoons show a declining trend except in the Eleventh Plan by moving up eight notches over the previous Plan, as indicated in the first chapter.

Some favourable aspects of growth have been that there is enough enthusiasm and enough incentive for private investment in agriculture as investment in agriculture went up from 12 percent in the Tenth Five Year Plan to 20 percent in the Eleventh Five Year Plan. But it has occurred more due to diversification of agriculture in to animal husbandry, horticulture, aqua and other allied sectors. Though we had worse drought in 2009–10 than 2002–03, we have been able to withstand it due to this diversification and the overall growth of the economy. Structural changes that need to be noted are that the number of large farmers has been declining during the last five years because they are abandoning agriculture and taking to either services or real estate sectors, because agriculture has become costly. They are, however, not abandoning land but leasing it out, causing the lessees to fend for themselves, and this has brought to fore the issues of tenant farming. The marginal farmers found more advantage in moving to the labour market, which promised higher wages than farming, and the small farmers found it difficult to cope with the 20–25 percent rise in labour costs in the costs of cultivation. The demographic dividend in the rest of the economy just does not exist in farming. The highest ever increase reported by financing institutions in credit left the figures suspect, with continuing suicides of farmers oppressed by usurious loans from moneylenders.

The farmer is, therefore caught in a scenario of limited access to land, with shrinking employment opportunities in the rural sector, forcing rural-urban migration, low level of infrastructure, high cost of cultivation, unremunerative prices for agricultural products, inadequate credit facilities, poor quality of inputs, poor extension services and the threat of cheaper imports of agricultural commodities at a time when the state appears to be withdrawing from active supportive interventions. Availability of adequate and timely credit can be of immense importance in widening the options facing the farmer and improving his ability to tackle all the changes that are underway in the agricultural sector.

Policy dilemmas are as follows:

1. Agricultural policy in India was a motley collection of piecemeal changes and legislative acts within an overall regulative mode.
2. The objective included protecting the consumers who were largely of modest means, and providing incentives for accelerated growth in production of food and industrial raw materials.

3. The mould of policies came in for a major change with the onset of liberalization in 1991, and soon thereafter, India became a signatory to the new world trade arrangement (under WTO), which for the first time included agriculture.
4. India's integration in to the world trade regime became a part of the agenda of reforms. The widely held notion that the Indian farmer was heavily protected and subsidized in a regulated regime has come in for serious scrutiny, and it is now held that the farmer is on the whole "taxed" rather than subsidized. Unabated inflation is the most regressive tax on the poor rather than the rich.

Figure 1.2: Technology subsidized inputs

A major dilemma for policymakers is the classic trade-off between growth and equity. Some key issues for agricultural policy are discussed below:

Crop Planning

A sustained effort has to be made to encourage farmers to take to crop planning, consistent with natural resource endowment. This would demand intensive extension efforts from both the State Departments of Agriculture and already well-developed research institutions. The time has come again when scientists, policymakers and economists have to work as a team. Peripatetic teams should be formed either with the initiative of the farmers' associations or the state governments or NGOs to work at the village and *mandal* levels for disseminating knowledge on crop planning and cultural practices. We have misdirected subsidies routed through the public distribution system, fertilizer industry and loan write-offs at the will of the politicians. Assured minimum price support has encouraged farmers to go in for foodgrain crops like paddy and wheat irrespective of the natural resources that are available for such crops. With 70 percent of the production in the hands of only medium and large farmers, and with small farmers growing crops mainly to sustain themselves and their families, it is obvious that the subsidies in the name of the small are reaching the big. This does not mean that we are doling out huge subsidies for the sector. But the subsidies that should be given at the input level are being given at the output-end making the sector inefficient. Unless there is a rethinking on these issues and we revisit our policies, it would be difficult to convince farmers about crop planning and a sustainable revival of agriculture.

Regeneration of the Natural Resource Base

Soil erosion and depletion of soil nutrients resulting from single crop cultivation or inefficient crop rotation is a major problem in many parts of the country. For example, in the Sangli-Satara-Kolhapur belt, sucrose yield of sugarcane has come down from 12 percent a decade and a half ago to 6 percent now, making the sugar industry uncompetitive. There is depletion of ground water resources in several parts of the country, including Punjab, Haryana, Andhra Pradesh, Karnataka, Tamil Nadu, etc, where the energy required for pulling out one unit of irrigable water has been on the increase. This is having a cascading effect on the energy sector with the farmers refusing to go for metering the energy consumption, whether paid or unpaid. Capital expenditure for regeneration of natural resources, both from the public and private sectors, was next to nothing during the last decade.

Bio-fertilization, penning of sheep and goats on farms in the pre-monsoon period, soil replenishments, washing of soil salinity in large patches across the length and breadth of the country, etc, to cite a few measures, deserve the attention of the farming community.

Land Equity Markets

This topic has been dealt with in Chapter 2 in greater detail.

Institutional Support System

Unlike anywhere else in the world, farm and allied sectors are looked after by at least 14 ministries and a host of bureaucratic organizations like Ministry of Agriculture; Ministry of Animal Husbandry, Dairy Development, and Fisheries; Ministry of Major and Medium Irrigation; Ministry of Cooperation; Ministry of Revenue, Relief and Rehabilitation; Ministry of Finance; Ministry of Food and Civil Supplies; Ministry of Marketing and Warehousing, at the state level, and Ministry of Agriculture and Cooperation; Ministry of Food Processing; Ministry of Finance; Ministry of Forests & Environment; Ministry of Commerce and Trade; Ministry of Food and Civil Supplies at the central government level. There is the State Planning Board and the Union Planning

Commission at the helm to decide on many issues that concern all these ministries. Each Ministry has its regulatory strings to apply on the farmer because each is an empire unto itself and there is no coordination among them at the beginning of the agriculture season. The Planning Commission ceased to be a coordination agency long back. It is content with preparing grandiose plans and allocating limited resources through discussions at the National Development Council. Exigencies of politics predominate economic necessities.

In agrarian states like Andhra Pradesh, a beginning could be made in reorganizing the ministries to start with, and bringing the departments of agriculture, horticulture and allied activities like animal husbandry, fisheries, that deal with production, cooperation, marketing, civil supplies and distribution under a single minister, who should have full comprehension and empathy for farmers. The organizational structure could be as follows:

Figure 1.3: Organizational Chart of the State Ministry of Agriculture

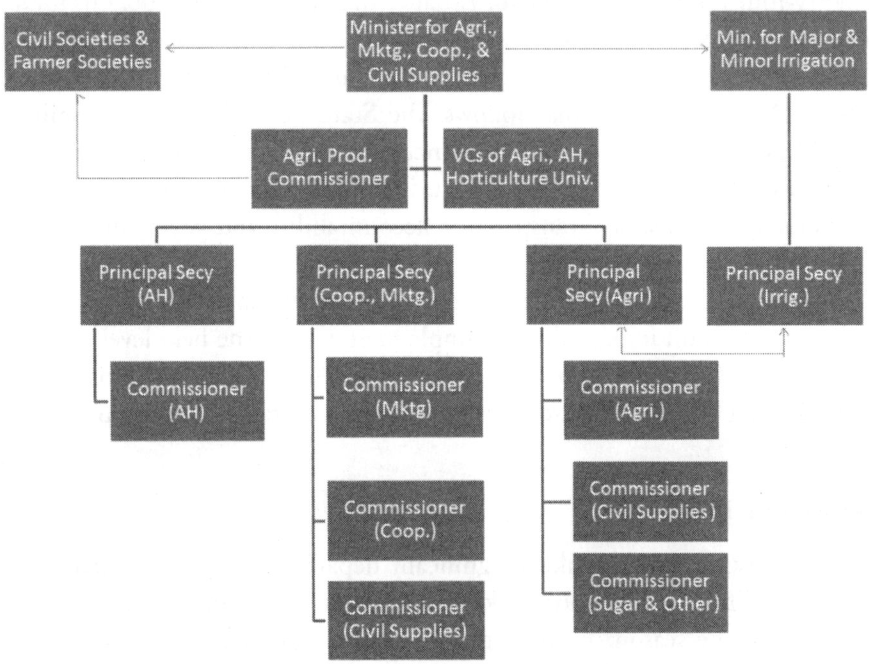

This would mean that the number of ministries at the state level would be reduced to one from the existing four. There is a peer level relationship between civil societies and, farmers' associations on one side, and the Minister for Irrigation on the other. Likewise, the Agriculture Production Commissioner would have a peer level relationship with the Vice Chancellors of the agriculture universities. At the beginning of the season, all the above functionaries would have a meeting with all the functionaries in the chart for a day or two. In this coordination meeting presided over by the Minister, Agriculture Production Commissioner who is of the rank of Additional Chief Secretary, is expected to be fully informed of all the links in the supply chain in production and value chain management in agriculture, right up to the distribution end, and would be in a position to format the decision making process depending upon the various issues that come up for discussion. The Minister can also invite the Principal Secretary (Energy) and Principal Secretary (Information Technology) for the half-yearly meetings to take into consideration the issues and facilitation that could come from them to the farmers during and off the season. Principal Secretary (Agriculture) should be the Member-Secretary for this coordination panel. He would draft the minutes within the next twenty-four hours and arrange for issuance of appropriate instructions for all these line departments to follow implicitly and the concerned departmental heads would be squarely responsible for any and all lapses in implementing them. During the week that follows, the State Level Bankers' Committee should be convened to cause the financial arrangements to be put in place. This mechanism would expand the burden of implementation on those who are actually responsible. Transparency, accountability and governance would significantly improve.

Whenever disasters occur, an emergency meeting shall be held to take a collective decision for coordinated implementation at the field level through the District Collectors. The Minister for Revenue would coordinate with the Minister for Agriculture in situations of natural calamities and other disasters.

Agriculture Budget

These measures would make a significant departure from each department pulling in different directions, making the farmers suffer both at the beginning and end of the season. Further, predominantly agrarian states like Andhra Pradesh, Tamil Nadu, Punjab, Haryana, and Karnataka (which has already started such initiatives) should put up an Annual Agriculture Budget every year preceded by presentation of Agriculture Survey of the State done by the agriculture, animal husbandry and horticulture universities. Agriculture budget would specify the direction of expenditure into subsidies, distribution and revenues that come from marketing cess and other sources, and the deficit or surplus that it projects. The farmers would know by the end of February every year, what the situation of the state is, to help them.

This would also help reduce unnecessary expenditure in multiple delivery points in meaningless directions.

1. This scenario would make one believe that the credit is a necessary but an insufficient condition to agricultural growth. Little or no attention was paid to the high transaction costs, administrative costs, quality of service, or to innovation in financial services for the poor.
2. It was further assumed that most farmers are too poor to save, and most rural financial markets are dominated by the moneylenders charging usurious rates of interest and also that the commercial bankers were too conservative to lend to agriculture, and more particularly, to small and marginal farmers, as also lease hold and tenant farmers. A pressing need has been felt to reshape agricultural policies in keeping with the new demands of the fast-changing economic environment. Credit for the farm sector continues to be a priority policy area.

The growing number of suicides by farmers in different parts of the country in recent years is largely the result of borrowing from non-institutional sources at very high rates of interest. This scenario led the RBI and the Government of India to look at "financial inclusion" as a necessary policy intervention at this point of the country's economic history.

1. Declining public investments in agriculture in the last two decades is the Indian farmers' greatest enemy, and this has undermined the future prospects of agriculture, since it is often complementary to private investment in agriculture.
2. Most private investment in agriculture is more "debt-driven" than "equity-driven" and this debt comes from both institutional and non-institutional lenders. 70 to 80 percent of capital investment went into just 10 states in the country—mostly irrigated tracts. These states are: Andhra Pradesh, Karnataka, Tamil Nadu, Kerala, Maharashtra, Gujarat, Punjab, Haryana, Uttar Pradesh and West Bengal. No doubt, there has been a slight shift in the rain fed areas fairly contributing to growth in agriculture rather than only the irrigated areas. As mentioned earlier, this is due to diversification in agriculture.

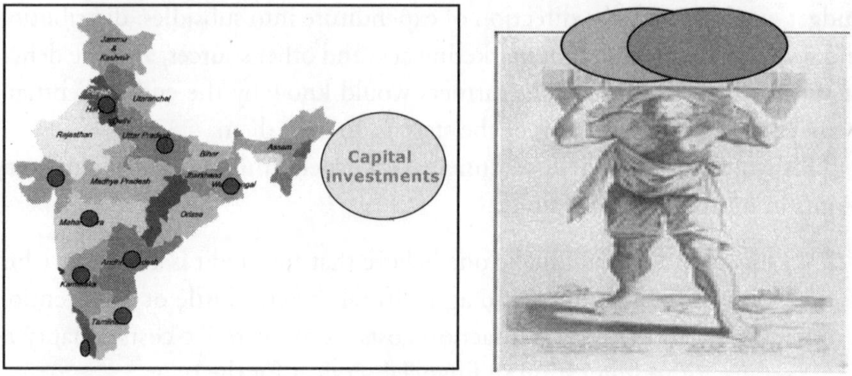

Figure 1.4

Still, there is enough scope for technological intervention in promoting higher and sustained growth in rain-fed agriculture in vast tracts. The drought-proofing efforts need to be stepped up.

1. In recent years, some substantial investments have been made in developing agricultural infrastructure in western India and in Andhra Pradesh. Some parts of this region support cereals and sugarcane, absorbing both surface and underground water resources in large measure. Cash crops like oil seeds and cotton are grown in these areas. Crop diversification in search of new riches could lead eventually to food deficits, as the population dependent on agriculture did not show substantial decline. (The decline in six decades of independent India is barely 10 percent.)
2. Storage deficiencies have become alarming and conspicuous.

Table 1.1: Certain key characteristics of operational holdings

	1960–61 (17th)	1970–71 (26th)	1981–82 (37th)	1991–92 (48th)	2003 (59th)
Number of operational holdings (in millions)	50.77	57.07	71.04	93.45	101.27
Percentage increase	–	12.4	24.5	31.5	8.4
Area operated (in million hectares)	133.48	125.68	118.57	125.10	107.65
Average area operated (in hectares)	2.63	2.20	1.67	1.34	1.06

Source: NSSO, Some Aspects of Operational Land Holdings in India, Various Rounds.

Table 1.2: Changes in the distribution size of operational holdings and operated area

Category of holdings	Percentage of operational holdings					Percentage of operated area				
	1960–61 (17th)	1970–71 (26th)	1981–82 (37th)	1991–92 (48th)	2003 (59th)	1960–61 (17th)	1970–71 (26th)	1981–82 (37th)	1991–92 (48th)	2003 (59th)
Marginal	39.2	45.8	56.0	62.8	69.1	6.8	9.2	11.5	15.6	22.6
Small	22.8	22.4	19.3	17.8	16.6	12.3	14.7	16.6	18.7	20.9
Semi-medium	19.8	17.7	14.2	12.0	9.2	20.7	22.6	23.6	24.2	22.5
Medium	14.8	11.0	8.6	6.1	4.3	31.2	30.5	30.1	26.4	22.2
Large	4.5	3.1	1.9	1.3	0.8	29.0	23.0	18.2	15.2	11.8
All sizes	100.0	100.0	100.0	100.0	100.0	100.0	100.0	100.0	100.0	100.0

Source: NSSO, Some Aspects of Operational Land Holdings in India, Various Rounds.

Employment Generation

Although the inherently unstable nature of agriculture justifies the presence of a large number of social safety nets, the largest safety net lies in providing sustainable livelihood opportunities in and around agriculture and in rural areas. The rural-urban connect emerges from the farm sector.

Information from various NSS surveys suggests that rural economy has seen sectoral diversification with the share of non-farm sector in employment increasing modestly during the last ten years. The work force shifted from agriculture to manufacturing and services. There has also been an increase in the range of services, with the traditional rural services sector based on community or caste, shifting to others. Mahatma Gandhi National Rural Employment Guarantee Act (MGNREGA) tilted the scales from productive employment to unproductive wage distribution, albeit with modest success in areas where the social audit has been effective. Non-farm employment in rural areas and agriculture growth has reported positive correlation in a few research studies.[1]

Employment elasticity (percent change in employment for 1 percent change in corresponding output) worked out by Aarif Waquif in his research study relating to South Asia, indicates that it was 0.5 in agriculture and manufacturing, 0.7 in services and 0.6 in economic infrastructure as per the related GDP growth components in 1997. If migration from the rural areas continues at the current pace with volatile growth in the manufacturing sector, the prospects of stable employment opportunities would vastly diminish. Therefore, policy thrust needs to be on enhancing positive externalities and reducing negative externalities. Improved rural infrastructure and reduced transaction costs hold the key. Government regulation that tends to raise transaction costs and prevent efficient private trade in agriculture commodities needs to be removed. Several small farmer families utilize their farm output for conversion into ready-to-eat foods although most of them do not conform to health and hygiene standards. While the earlier Development of Women and Children in Rural Areas (DWCRA) and self-help groups endeavoured to empower these vulnerable groups and reasonably succeeded in such efforts, these have not proved to be replicable and sustainable. Another window of opportunity became available for Multinational Corporations (MNCs) to use these groups to take their products at the lowest cost to rural markets while the MNCs did not make any effort to change the production pattern to suit demanding market standards.

Increasing value addition in the production and marketing of agricultural produce should be a major thrust of future agricultural policy for employment generation in non-farm sector at one end and retention of employment interest in the farm sector at the other. There are several links in the value chain that link production on the farm to the last retail point to reach the consumer. The production chain and the value chain extend from the farmer's field to the retailer's shelf through a set of links that include post-harvest technologies and marketing interventions.

In the wake of WTO compulsions and the fast transforming demand scenarios in the rural and semi-urban areas, the other spectrum reflects a demand-shift in favour of quality products, ready-to-eat food, branded products, health and hygiene-backed products, etc. The last decade has witnessed a phenomenal growth in self-help groups, particularly of the women supported by the government sponsored DWCRA scheme, NGOs, Non-Banking Financial Companies (NBFCs), and indirectly assisted by funding institutions like the Small Industries Development Bank of India (SIDBI) and NABARD. We have more than 5 lakh villages and around 97,000 Primary Agricultural Cooperatives Societies (PACS) craving reforms and crying for assistance, both financial and managerial.

There is a broad realization that value addition to agriculture would take place only through agro-industries and agri-businesses. The UPA Government has announced incentives for setting up agro-enterprises with support from the banks and financial institutions. All these efforts are still in embryonic stages. Failures of earlier institutional mechanisms and the tardy progress in the new initiatives, the jobless growth in agriculture and industry wherever growth occurred, reflect the need for modern management and promotional ability as essential managerial inputs to the creation and utilization of infrastructure under Bharat Nirman that provides knowledge connectivity to rural India. This programme of rural infrastructure centres on irrigation, rural roads, rural water supply, rural housing, rural electrification and rural telephone connectivity. Development practitioners have long recognized the need for building physical and knowledge connectivity in parallel that forms the essence of Provision of Urban Amenities in Rural Areas (PURA).

A.P.J. Abdul Kalam, in his inaugural address to the Second Mission 2007 Convention and at the 93rd Indian Science Congress (2006), opined, "The physical connectivity of the village clusters through quality roads and transport; electronic connectivity through telecommunication with high bandwidth fibre optic cables reaching the rural areas from urban cities and through Internet kiosks; knowledge connectivity through education, skill training for farmers, artisans and craftsmen and entrepreneurship programmes. These three connectives will lead to economic connectivity through starting of enterprises with the help of PACS, commercial and rural banks, Microfinance Institutions (MFIs) and marketing of products."

The Village Knowledge Centres (VKCs) will assist various schemes reinforced by the government, such as the MGNREGA, National Rural Health Mission, Anthyodaya Anna Yojana, the universalization of the Integrated Child Development Services, Sarva Siksha Abhiyan, Rajiv Gandhi National Drinking Water Mission, and others. The VKCs will also contribute towards the up liftment of the marginalized, including Scheduled Castes, the Scheduled Tribes, children, women and other minorities. Further, the VKCs will act as the last-mile windows for disseminating government information to citizens mandated under the Right to Information Act (RTI) 2005, proposed by the UPA Government. M.S. Swaminathan Foundation has successfully created such centres in the earlier tsunami-affected villages.

The "New Deal for India" would require integration of various schemes with their implementation, overseen by a responsible institution with a sense of commitment. Linkages of traditional village producers to the outside world are performed by traders whose interests generally run counter to the interests of the producers. There is an inherent urge on the part of bureaucrats to create new institutions instead of reviving falling angels. The PACS, whose revival got a shot in the arm with the implementation of the recommendations of Vaidyanathan Committee, can fulfil this need provided the two key deficiencies afflicting them—managerial and governance are tackled statutorily. The advantage with the PACS is that these can take all types of activities that contribute to growth of the entire rural economy; they can store seeds and supply; they can extend credit and recover it with ease because of the limited area of operation; they can store the output—both in cold storage and grain and seed godowns; they can set up marketing infrastructure by opening a spot exchange with farmers as members; they can market the output; they can participate in public distribution mechanism; they can effectively set up processing houses and laboratories and other infrastructure for packing and transport—all under one roof, and their existing bylaws provide for such elaborate interventions. But then, the question that arises is why did they fail thus far? They have been looked at as windows of credit and delivery channels of inputs, and only in some exceptional areas, they performed the rest of the functions. Cooperatives have proved successful in milk production, procurement, processing, storage and sale, for example, AMUL. The SHGs in Andhra Pradesh registered under the AP Mutually Aided Cooperative

Societies Act, 1995, similarly succeeded in providing livelihood opportunities by providing end-to-end services to their members. They created a record of sorts in procurement of maize in Nizamabad and Karimnagar districts, and its storage and sale to the advantage of the farming community. In the last two years, they have even been distributing fertilizers. Cooperative societies set up under the guidance of another promotional organization saw the emergence of end-to-end value chain management of groundnut production in Anantapur district. The farmers produce oil, chickens, masala nuts, etc, in hygienically packed packets. Credit is thus just one of the many components of its services. How does this all happen? The societies must decide to appoint professionals on competitive salaries as secretaries of these societies to run them in a professional manner, maintain accounts and other records with transparency and accountability, and have the accounts audited by professional auditors approved by their boards that definitely meet at half-yearly intervals or at more frequent intervals, when policy issues need discussion. But the decrepit PACS, in large numbers they are (97,000), needed more oxygen than the inefficient pumping done thus far, with better recruitment, management and financial supports that came through the revival package announced in 2005 and only partly released thus far (out of Rs 15,000 crore announced, only about Rs 8,000 crore has been released thus far). The states that have received money under the revival package did not seriously consider the package as a revival effort and reformation of agriculture itself. It has not considered the business development plans as the seedbeds of economic resurgence of the rural areas. There are more than 3,000 cooperative officers in Andhra Pradesh, whose game plan is to please either the politician or the boss or both, rather than development of the cooperatives. Their performance, if judged based on revival of the PACS as mentioned above, their resurgence would have seen the resurgence of rural India and provision of sustainable rural livelihoods. Most PACS, being computerized under a specific revival plan and accounting procedures, have also moved in tandem with those in the commercial banks. Technology would finally integrate the entire financial system at the micro level with the macro level. Payment and settlement systems would cover these entities quickly. Development of healthy cooperative credit system is integral to stability of the Indian financial system.

This should be also viewed from the context of the scams in large companies in several sectors from retail to software to telecom to banks, both within the country and across the globe. The advantage of a cooperative form of organization is that it has checks and balances built into the structure, with member-participation and member-control. The present malaise of these cooperative structures is poor management compounded by inefficient and even maleficent governance. These two defects can be overcome with certain amendments to the statutes by both the state and central governments. Although some sound bites have come in the shape of amendment to the Constitution—97th Constitution Amendment Act 2011 and model governance code, dilution of the role of the registrar and government through more effective Mutually Aided Cooperative Societies Acts in the states (only 9 states in the country have such laws), these are hibernating either in the walls of the state governments. We already have successes in milk and sugar cooperatives. Why should we not replicate the successes with depoliticization of PACS in credit?

Project Concept

Economic empowerment of vulnerable groups in rural areas would depend upon the provision of necessary wherewithal within their existing domestic environs instead of shifting them to common work places. Agro-processing therefore assumes critical importance in this regard.

The agro-processing industry is critically placed in the economy as its development contributes significantly not only to the value chain but also achieves a number of development objectives such as promoting rural-urban link and speeding up rural industrialization, raising farmers' incomes and increasing exports.

There are several agricultural products that can serve as raw material for the food processing industry, as a wide variety of processed products can be made with their input. Rice, wheat, maize, sugarcane and soybean, are some of the products that can enter into the value addition chain. Several types of fruits and vegetables have immense potential to be processed for domestic and global markets.

Growth in demand is projected for frozen/dehydrated/canned fruits and vegetables, fruit juices/concentrates/pulps, pickles, jams, jellies, squashes, etc, apart from ready-to-eat vegetables. A significant share of consumption in developed markets—almost 60 percent in the US/ Canada/ Europe/ South East Asia—is for fruits and vegetables in processed form. In Philippines, Indonesia, Thailand and even in mainland China, it is the SHGs that are engaged in these activities most successfully.

The constraints that the farmer faces in the agro-processing link of the supply/value chain are related to lack of adequate information about the possibilities of processing agricultural products, the importance of price and quality. The financial constraint can be overcome if the PACS can be directly financed by the State Cooperative Bank with 70 percent refinance from NABARD, as participation in this sector requires considerable amounts of investment. The volumes would eventually make the PACS the most viable entity in the financial sector. When it took two decades of continuous recapitalization of public sector banks to usher in reforms in the banking sector, thanks to the two reports of M. Narasimham (one on financial sector and another on the banking sector), and unhesitating support to a few large private sector banks under the principle—too big to fail—could become a credible act in the eyes of Parliament. Can we not pick up the courage to clean up the cooperative system from excessive political interference and extend financial support for at least a decade to come? Can we not build checks and balances for such supports to ensure that they become vehicles of employment and growth because, they are democratic institutions? Can we not develop a sense of urgency to bring about legal and regulatory reforms in the cooperative sector? Can this not form an important agenda for the NDA and the Twelfth Five Year Plan? Time is ripe now more than ever. The cycle of empowering the poor centres round the cooperatives as mentioned in the chart that follows.

Figure 1.5: The Cycle of Empowerment of the Rural Poor

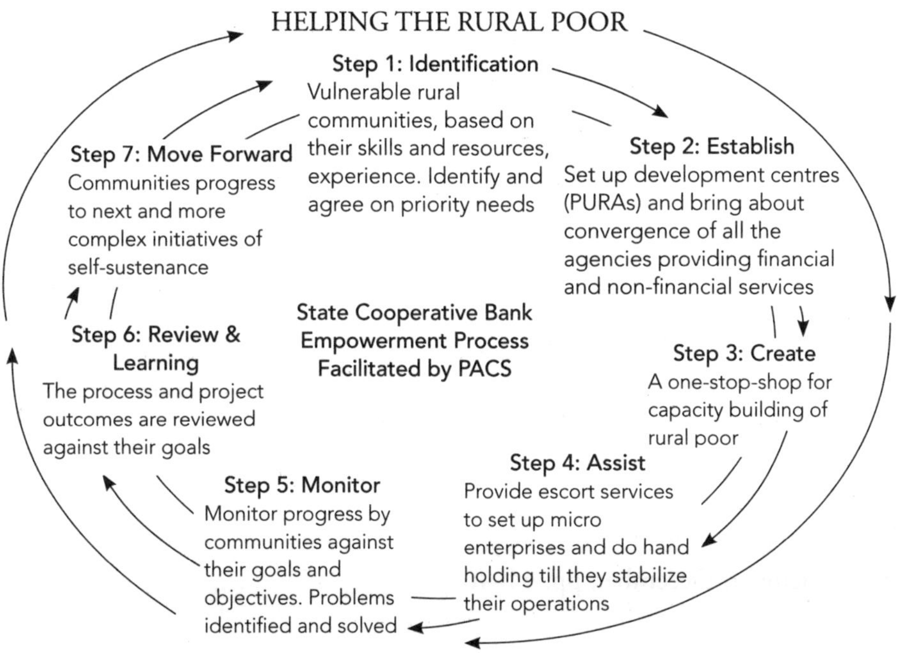

Figure 1.6: Linkage Model

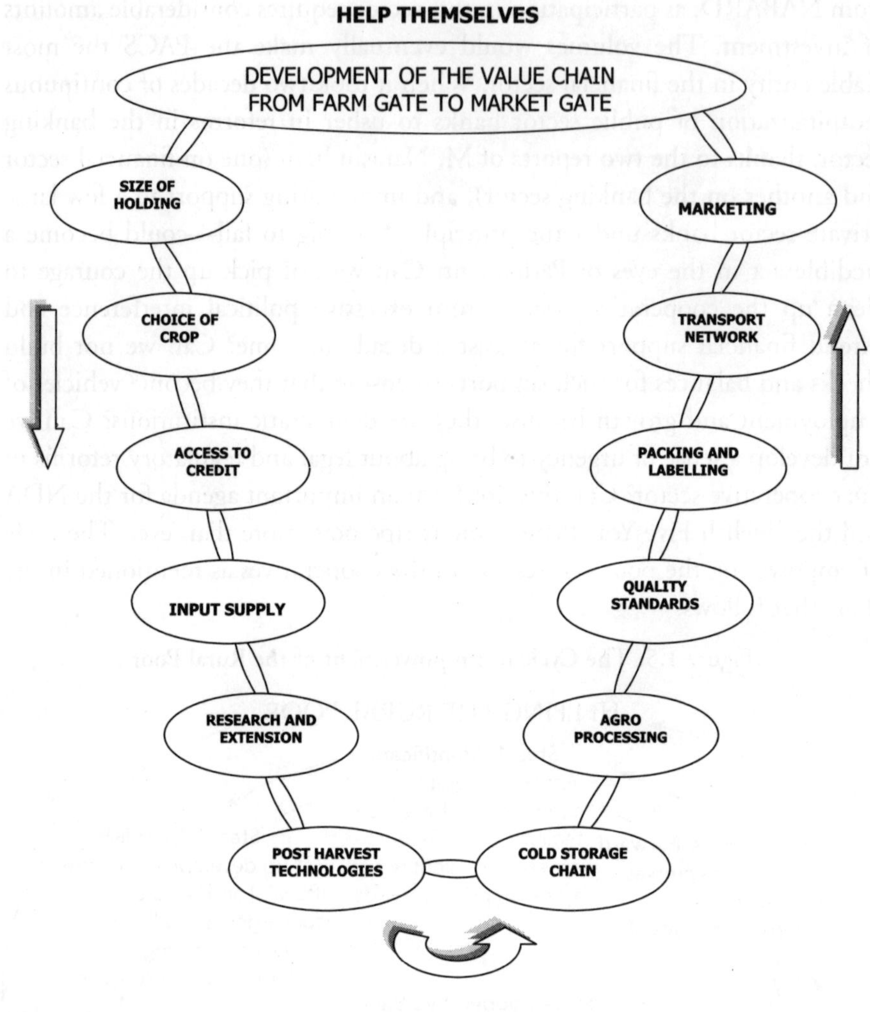

Notes

1. A. Kundu, 2004, "Country Study on Right to Food", India: Food and Agriculture Organization.

Reference

Yerram Raju, B. 2011, *Inclusion Journal,* Skoch Development Foundation, October–December, pp. 44–46.

LAND ISSUES

CHAPTER 2

Land Equity Markets: Shape of the Future

Land markets in India are primitive. Buyers and sellers of land depend on the Almighty and transact land businesses. About 50 percent of the operational holdings in any state are plagued by legal disputes. These disputes arise on account of ownership. Sub-division and fragmentation of land holdings is a natural phenomenon that takes place in India on account of the excessive emphasis on inheritance rights. Over and above this, there are lots of areas where the state itself is the owner. Due to either misuse or abuse of power, revenue authorities have allowed encroachments into the state's properties. The encroachers have been given titles by default in several cases. Then, there were land reforms. Defective implementation of land reforms has again led to conferment of titles in the hands of those that used them for their own purposes. Such land also got titles conferred over a period of time. Apart from all these complications, the mafia and the politically powerful had their own ways of acquiring land and retaining their position and it has no relationship either with legitimacy or legality. Lands were partitioned for a variety of purposes and these did not go on record. There is no state in India where the land records are updated and all the latest mutations carried out.

Though land constitutes an important factor of production, reforms in land markets are yet to be touched. Reforms in the agricultural sector, viewed as part of the reforms in the factors of production that contribute to nearly one third of the GDP, are in their incipient stage. Agricultural policy changes during the past decade have altered the comparative advantages of landlords and tenants. Today, one will find more and more tenants cultivating farm lands than the owners, despite the number of operational holdings showing consistent increase without corresponding increase in the area of operational holdings. The Government of India and the different state governments spent more than Rs 500 crores on Computerization of Land Records (CLR) during the past ten years; still, not much has happened on this front. This is because of the vested interests that would like to perpetuate the present status.

Limited initiatives of finance for land purchases from credit institutions are severely constrained by the lack of rate of return and a similar fate befalls the credit for farming operations. With land being an important factor of production, imperfections in land markets will lead to serious imbalances in agricultural production; hence, investments in the CLR on the public-private participation model should not be delayed.

Consolidation of Land Holdings

With regard to the Agreement on Agriculture in the WTO, the farmers need to look at agriculture not just as a subsistence occupation, but as a commercial one. This would make consolidation of land holdings a viable alternative, which, however, would not infringe on the basic rights of the farmer on the asset he holds. There are arguments and counter-arguments to the size neutrality in keeping this land as an economic asset. Still, there is no doubt that a larger land holding is more amenable for superior technology adoption. The recent amendment to the Companies Bill, providing for producer cooperatives to reorganize themselves into companies, is a step in the right direction.

The shrinking size of land holdings in India on the one hand, and, fragmentation on the other, which led the farmers to hold land in disaggregated parcels spread over different revenue villages, made management of agriculture an uneconomic proposition. Therefore, the consolidation of land holdings was thought of.

Although the programme of consolidation of holdings was suggested to state governments five decades ago, it was only implemented in Punjab, Haryana, and partly, Uttar Pradesh. Consolidation would also help generate environment-friendly farm operations, for example, the effects of aquaculture on agriculture in freshwater cultivating farms in some states.

The societal impact is a significant factor. Caste barriers continue to impinge on consolidation efforts. Neutralizing this factor would appear to be impossible currently with the help of any policy instrumentation. The only way out is through the use of participatory mechanisms, and also, sometimes, a long wait. This policy of, "let things simmer down, they will take care of themselves" has worked in some cases. Viewed in this perspective, what should be the objectives of policy?

Objectives of Land Consolidation Policy

The objectives of policy on consolidation of land holdings shall be to:

1. Make farming operations commercial.
2. Facilitate implementation of higher level of technology in farming operations.
3. Provide for flexibility in dealing with land markets.
4. Protect and preserve the rights of farmers to the assets and production processes.

There would, however, appear to be no scope for attaining such objectives without some radical thinking on the subject. Land records cannot be updated on a regular and continuing basis. Neither farmers nor policymakers welcome such consolidation measures. But the country has to move forward and the farmers should have flexibility and easy access to land markets.

Land Equity Markets

Would it not be wiser to convert the parcel of land the farmer holds into share scrips in his hands, so that land equity markets can emerge? Such markets could respond to all the above issues in one go. One may wonder how. Imagine a farmer with just 1 acre or 100 cents holding 100 share certificates, where the share value gets fixed with some basic price for a cent of land across the state with a multiplier for coefficients like, (a) soil status; (b) agro-climatic zone; (c) type of irrigation he commands, and; (d) the nature of crops grown round the year on the farm. If this scrip is tradeable in land markets excessively created at the state/sub-state levels, then, if the land gets partitioned, the owner can sell the scrip to the extent of such transaction. The more it gets divided, the less the value of the scrip. Since no farmer would like to see his scrip going down, he would like to seek consolidation. Transferring the share certificate to new owners would be faster and easier than physically sub-dividing the land. This could also facilitate the floating of agricultural companies. Loans can be raised against land-share certificates in the state/sub-state land markets that could function under the control of the existing stock exchanges, with separate sets of rules that could be framed by SEBI. This idea can be discussed by farmers' associations and problems arising from such discussions ironed out. Thereafter, a comprehensive document can be worked out, giving the modalities of the instruments and institutions of land equity markets through a think tank that could be set up at the state level.

The effect of this would be that state revenue departments would be marginalized. But, resistance can be dealt with a well-thought out strategy. Such markets can eventually be in a position to raise loans from banks/ lending institutions. New financial instruments and their derivatives may also shape up, eventually giving rise to a vibrant agricultural economy without burdening the exchequer, on one hand, while the surpluses could come under the tax net on the other.

A Strategy for Sustainability for the Poor

The time is ripe now for structural innovations in our farm strategies. The poor have to be enabled through strategies which lead to the elimination of poverty over a period of time.

A suggested strategy is to take a big tranche of 100–200 hectares, making every landholder there a shareholder of a company formed by the constituents. The equity contributions will be on the basis of land holding of the owner. These owners of farm lands constitute the promoters of the company. The 100 hectare tranche will be the project site. The crop-mix will be decided on the basis of the potential of the farm lands in terms of the soil, water and environmental resources. A suitable agro-industry/agri-business venture will be set up to match the project potential envisaged. The financial resources for the project will be mobilized from the funding institutions like NABARD for agriculture and allied activities and SIDBI/Industrial Finance Corporation of India (IFCI) or venture capital for the agro-industry/agri-business venture. The margin requirements will be mobilized from the pre-investment annual output of the farm lands. Working capital requirements will be mobilized through the commercial banking institutions as per existing norms. The funding institutions will have to relax the existing debt/equity norms for such ventures, say 1:5:1. The farm plan can be export-oriented, in which case, the industry can be linked to a packaging unit. The farmer shareholders will continue their farming activity, but on the revised farm plan agreed to in the general body meeting of the newly constituted company. Infrastructure plan for the company, in terms of field channels, roads, power, etc, will have to be carefully prepared. If it involves earmarking of farm lands for the purpose, the compensation should be equitable among the shareholders with no reduction in the equity holding. The approval for the project should be accorded by the general body meeting of the shareholders of the company unlike in any other company where the Chief Executive will be empowered to decide such matters. Integration of infrastructure, farming, industry and trade will thus become possible, and a structural change in the economy will eventually be possible without any reduction in the dependence of the economy on agriculture on one hand, and provision of employment opportunities in the rural hinterland on the other. If these suggestions require modification of the Company Act, they have to be engineered appropriately. Depending on the size of investment, the company can go for public issue on a restricted scale or in a constricted area. In effect, this is the cooperative company.

The second strategy worth pursuing for promoting agri-business and agro-industry linkage with farming operations to directly benefit the poor is as follows:

Nearly half the country's farm lands are under mortgage to the financial institutions and the latter have more than 3 lakh accounts in courts for recovery. Most of the lands mortgaged cannot be sold easily either in private sale or public auction, for want of bidders. The actual value is much more than the decreed debt. The government may liaise with the banks in this regard. The newly constituted Recovery Tribunals, when they start functioning, may expedite the issue of decrees in favour of the lending agency. In that case, the realization of decretal amounts would depend upon the speed with which the decrees become executable. For a change, the state governments, through their SC/BC Corporations, can buy up such land and distribute it among the weaker sections with certain specified terms and conditions. By following a project approach, these lands can be converted into good agro-industrial use.

This raises the question about the type of industries and activities that can be sustained. Agriculture is a seasonal activity; every crop and every product has a season. The underemployment in farming operations can be made up for the agro-industry if the farm labour themselves are trained to operate the industry, because of least displacement of labour in the 100 hectare owned company. The shareholder himself is a worker. The yield of most of the agricultural produce is obtained twice/thrice in a year. During the off-season, these products have to be stored properly for serving the needs of the agro-industry or processing industry. The risks consequent to shorter shelf-life and the fluctuating prices have also to be properly insulated. It is estimated that approximately Rs 4,000 crores worth vegetable and fruit production in the country gets wasted due to poor storage facilities.

Several pulping units/fruit processing units work only for two or three months in a year because of the seasonal availability of inputs. The low capacity utilization of such units can be countered only through development of alternative input supplies matched by appropriate machining modifications. In such units, the raw materials with limited shelf-life have to be connected into semi-finished goods for storage and conversion into finished products subsequently. This would involve a careful working out of the operation cycle where the work-in-process will be for a longer duration. The conventional working out of working capital requirements will be detrimental to the profitability of operations.

Such complexes should be encouraged in respect to products where value addition can be significantly high. Export markets can be exploited with proper branding, packaging, advertising and pricing. The dichotomous situation that has to be combated is that the price of raw materials is determined by internal forces of demand and supply while those of the finished products will be dependent on external forces of demand and supply.

The setting up of a cooperative company along the lines suggested above should lead to an enlightened debate for converting it into a sustainable and implementable project.

CHAPTER 3

Land Information System: A Powerful Tool for Development

In a country like India, where almost 70 percent of the population is still dependent on land in one way or the other, and, where about 30 percent of the GDP is factored from agriculture, it is necessary that we should have proper Land Information Systems. Even after fifty years of independence, it is a pity that we should still be discussing how to put such a system in place.

Land Information System (LIS) refers to a well-networked information system covering a wide range of spatial information that includes data on land, water, weather, environment and socio-economic aspects. Growth of population on a static land base always leads to expanded land markets with monopsonic price pressures. Therefore, sourcing tools available under information technology for improving the highly congested land markets becomes imperative. Both administrators and users take recourse to efficient LIS that incorporates data collection, updation, dissemination and distribution. It involves integrating system objectives with the users' goals.

Users of LIS are categories of people or institutions who share common interest in a piece of land, be it an individual plot, an area under the occupation of a community, a natural conversion area, a region or a country. All groups, having interest in land, are concerned with ownership, rights, restrictions and responsibilities on the land. The government (revenue administration), the owners and lessees of land, lenders and insurers are the principal users of the LIS.

Need for a Land Information System

Nearly 20 registers are being maintained by the Revenue Department, the actual number varying from state to state. Different systems of land management also exist across the states although they broadly fall into the Ryotwari and Inamdar systems. The various registers and records are again known by different names in all these states. The principal records are:

1. Village maps (*Tippans* in the erstwhile Nizam's regime, which extends to parts of Andhra Pradesh, Karnataka and Maharashtra) indicate the village and field boundaries in graphic form, not necessarily drawn to any uniform scale.
2. Field measurement books(*Khasra*) are indexes to the map, usually indicating the changes in the field boundaries, their area, particulars of tenure holders, type of irrigation, area under cropping, other uses of land, etc.
3. Record of Rights (ROR) that reflects the names and classes of tenure of all occupants. The ROR by itself was not a title until the state governments passed a separate enactment for the purpose. The diversities in tenure, language differences, cultural practices, methods of field measurement, etc., make the exercise of development of suitable software difficult. In addition, if the mutations were to be carried out on an on-going basis and these can arise by way of family partitions, gifts, sub-divisions, fragmentations, sale and purchase, then these need authentication and acceptance by the administration and stakeholders respectively.

LIS is broadly classified into three categories:

1. Geologic Information: Its primary interest is in the nature, size, shape, and origin of landforms, rock, minerals and soils.
2. Economic Information: This deals with land classification, land use and inventory, such as irrigation, crops, pastures, forests, communities, transport routes, communications, navigation, etc.
3. Legal Information: This originates from legal objectives wherein land rights, settlement, administration, land registration and taxation are dealt with.

In the context of economic development, economic and legal information are of greater concern as both are inter-related. Cadastral surveys systematically record land rights, and can produce registers of land holdings or an inventory of land areas, land uses and classifications and also help determine tax assessments from the land.

Drought-prone areas need to be addressed on a different level. The recent thrust given to those in different parts of the country has been showing signs of reasonable success. The first and foremost of these strategies relate to soil and water conservation. This can best be tackled through integrated watershed management, linked with rationalization of land use according to topography. Cadastral surveys help significantly in the identification of catchment watersheds and diversion into sub- and micro-watersheds. They facilitate optimum utilization of the surface irrigation system through development of tanks, harnessing the water runoff, natural springs and life irrigation system in catchment areas of rivers.

Crop diversification, horticulture and floriculture development could also be planned in a systematic manner, with the participation of farmers in all the related key decisions, as farmers have relevant information gleaned through cadastral surveys.

The very fact that even the state government of Andhra Pradesh, where a ROR Act has been effectively brought into force, had to contend with the terrain rights of the tribals of West Godavari, Khammam and Adilabad districts, speaks of two issues: (a) inadequacies of the legislation, and; (b) usufructuary rights of the possessors. While the Andhra Pradesh Government took the lead in both legislation and implementation, there is a long way to go. India is a land of a large number of small holdings, continually subjected to further fragmentation and subdivisions, making them uneconomic day by day. These small operational holdings contribute to just 25 percent of the total agricultural production. We have terrains which are undulated, plain and uneven, whose contribution to production is also uneven. We have huge river basins again, with problems connected to river corridor management. These problems are reflected in the contribution of various states to agricultural production. Eleven states contribute to 87 percent of agricultural production in the country. It is these states which consume the largest quantum of resources and inputs. They exclude states like Orissa, Bihar, eastern Uttar Pradesh, the 7 sisters in the North-East and Madhya Pradesh, among others. The states named above have the most productive soils, vast water resources and hardworking farmers. But the credit required for putting these productive resources does not flow there for the simple reason that the financing institutions cannot identify the farmer with a particular land holding that he owns and/or cultivates. Further, the only male river of India, the Brahmaputra, fancifully floods most of the North-East at least twice a year, and, in the process, shifts the topography of several villages. Likewise, even the Ganges, when it floods the states of

Bihar and parts of West Bengal, as also eastern Uttar Pradesh, dismembers the piece or parcel of land a farmer has been cultivating. This puts the cultivating farmer at the mercy of a mighty landlord or politician, who provides him with an oral right to cultivate and enjoy only as much right over his own produce as the former chooses to part with. This perpetual dependence could have been done away with, had the LIS been available with those states.

Prerequisites for Establishing a Good LIS

Legal, administrative, technical and judicial reforms are crucial and they all impinge on the registration system. Some states such as Andhra Pradesh and Karnataka kept the following aims for reforms to the registration system:

1. Transparent pricing system.
2. Providing legal protection to rightful claimants of property.
3. Contributing to quick, safe, simple transfer of establishment or cancellation of rights.
4. Quick and easy delivery of titles registered to the rightful owners.

To ensure that the equity considerations are not bypassed by the government in the event of a farmer losing his farm holding in a natural disaster, the state government should have information on the following aspects in the pre-disaster situation:

1. Location and size of the land holding.
2. Name of the head of the household at the time of mutation.
3. Names of other family members with their ages.
4. Types of soil.
5. Crops grown with their yields.
6. Land cess.
7. Irrigation cess.

Whenever a disaster occurs, it is but natural that these farmers look to the state government to relocate them and rehabilitate them in the new habitats. While allocating land, depending on the above basic information, the state government can allocate a piece or parcel of land that has similar production potential.

Another important area where the LIS can help is in the resolution of disputes between the landed parties.

The third and most important area is in the field of land reforms. In the past, land reforms were viewed with the basic objective of providing the cultivator a right to own the piece of land he tills. Claims and counter claims exist in regard to redistribution of land among large landholders, tillers, shareholders and tenants. The process of land reforms, even in the communist-ruled state of West Bengal, remains incomplete. But such transformation of rights has always been riparian. However, for India to emerge as a major export earner in farm products, there is a need to consolidate holdings to gain economies of size. At the same time, no farmer would like to lose his foothold on the piece of land he owns.

Information Technology in LIS

Information technology should provide the administration a truly automated land records system, integrating ROR and cadastral maps that should conform to the numerous rules and regulations in vogue. It should provide accuracy and efficiency and eliminate the scope for manipulation and malpractice. It should make the system useful for all segments of government administration and citizens, within the confines of security and confidentiality.

The software on land records should integrate the textual RORs, cadastral maps, and other documents maintained by various revenue officials, that together form the LIS, regional language output, geographical information system tools that operate on digital maps and data conversion, cleaning, updation and audit. It should provide for adequate user-defined security for the entire data and facilitate access to all citizens with convenience and ease of operation.

Land data can be integrated with citizenship data and commercial data, so that at one kiosk, a citizen can access a birth or death certificate, nativity and caste certificates, payment systems for various facilities that the government provides, information for crop planning and management by the farmers in due course, with marginal self-generated investments.

CHAPTER 4

Land Systems Need Unconventional Solutions

Introduction

Despite the optimism in growth and a structural shift in the economy reducing the share of agriculture to 16–17 percent at the national level, the liberal reforms ushered in from the 1990s have not benefited the farm sector, and property rights continue to be under strain. The nexus between agriculture and politics remains an untangled web. Recently, Justice Laxman Rao, in a symposium on property rights, mentioned that the right to property incorporated as a fundamental right in the Indian Constitution, ceased to be "fundamental" and remained "constitutional". Right to Land continues to be the main constituent of property because it is still a means of livelihood, and the value of land has wide disparities between the rural and urban. It is as much a source of power as the cause of litigation, with as many as three million cases lying unresolved in the courts at all tiers. The state in most cases is either a plaintiff or defendant. Large-scale acquisitions or encroachments on land belonging to the small and marginal farmers took place in this country. Corruption has its roots in land deals. In the rural areas, subdivision and fragmentation of holdings has made operational holdings highly uneconomic. While it is true that the size of the holding was not a constraint in reaping the economies of farming in Japan and China, in India, it is the land system that acts as a constraint. Small land holdings are denying the farmers access to technology, quality inputs, mechanization, post-harvesting facilities, integrated approach to farming and market intelligence, as also bargaining power in the economy. Many small and marginal farmers chose to take on lease neighbouring lands for cultivation, and, as a result, they became tenants. In most irrigated tracts in Andhra Pradesh, 80 percent of operational holdings are under leasehold. The serious limitation for further progress in agriculture, and for increasing farmers' income, therefore, is lack of economies of scale, at least in India. Tenant-cultivators cannot access credit as neither the Group Loaning of 1970s, nor its latest avatar the joint liability farming scheme by NABARD-found acceptance with the primary lender. All the earlier experiments, like joint farming societies and cooperative farming, failed. The farmer is caught in the vicious circle of low productivity, lower income and lower investment, leading back to low productivity and perpetual marginalization. Some states attempted digitization of land records, for example, *bhoomi*, *bhu bharati*, etc. Without the cadastral survey and mutations, these digitization efforts have more problems than solutions, and such surveys, carried out more than sixty years ago, are expensive. Yet, they are still to attain reliability in the hands of the owner or tenant. Tenancy rights are beyond reach for the moment. The problem exists in land tenures and the solution has to be sought there. Extraordinary problems require extraordinary solutions.

There is no alternative to providing economies of scale for our farmers, to integrate farming with the markets and make them the owners of the value chain in order to increase incomes. There was an aborted attempt by the Andhra Pradesh Government, aimed at consolidating of holdings on voluntary basis to maximize benefits to farmers. It went into a spiral because of the attached 'cooperative' tag, and the policymakers' intentions were suspect in the wake of large-scale commercialization of acquired lands in the name of Special Economic Zones (SEZ)s. Integrated farming with animal husbandry, fisheries, sericulture, horticulture, post-harvest operations and processing, with value addition taking place at the doorstep of the farmers, is the only solution. This requires projectization at the village level.

New Approach

The new initiative aims at (1) increased production and productivity; (2) reasonable remuneration for produce in time; (3) value addition; (4) linking production with processing and marketing within compact areas; (5) better access to credit; (6) structuring a farmer-centric and farmer-participated reform in a novel fashion; etc. Most people agree that flexibility in dealing with land issues in a manner that does not hurt the interests of farmers and also providing incentives for the next generation to continue farming, holds the key to reform agenda in agriculture. This new approach should be able to provide an alternative to the not-so-successful earlier initiatives by joint cooperative farming societies, contract farming and producer companies, formed around a few agricultural products.

The Scheme I proposal seeks to promote participation by all farmers and persons with other occupations on the basis of a *pari pasu* charge on their assets—both land and houses—and proportional returns to the participants. The society/community, in other words the general body, would have the usufructuary right on the land of all members for implementing the new initiative. In other words, x,y,z farmers owning a,b,c tenures of land individually would pool together their lands for their own long-term benefit and improved economic status, where the community would decide on the land use planning for the most optimal returns. The land holding that the farmer agrees to vest with the community/society would be converted into a non-tradable but alienable scrip.

Valuation of Lands

There would be issues relating to valuation of lands, like road-side lands, wet lands, lands having minor irrigation structures, undulated lands, lands with terrain differences, soil textures, and so on. All the lands in a pool, or in a society, therefore, would have differences in valuation on varying parameters being applied. A computer model could solve this issue. The value of land could be decided based on consensus, as is being implemented in the case of Project Affected Persons under some projects. The voting rights will be proportionate to the shareholding, unlike in cooperatives where each person would hold only one vote. Non-land owners who are admitted into the society would have a single vote.

The Share Certificates represent the title to the property held by the individual member and are transferable, preferably to another member of the Society with the approval of the general body or its authorized board. The owner does not forsake his right over the piece of land he owns but joins others in enhancing the value of the land he owns. He can, in times of need, sell his piece or parcel of land at the market price but the transferee gets the ownership right duly recorded at the society in his name through the registry maintained by the Society or the Village Panchayat that is in command of the usufruct right. Land is one asset that cannot be taken away as another commodity and gets value only when used with the power of endowment it inherently possesses.

Avoiding Subdivision and Fragmentation

What happens in the process is that the land is not divided without, at the same time disturbing the hereditary rights to the property owned on one side and the production patterns on the other. Limited resources like water, soil health, etc, would be protected for optimal utilization. Other ancillary activities like animal husbandry, horticulture, fisheries etc, would mitigate the risks arising from crop losses.

The general body consists of all the farmers and non-farmers and it is they who collectively own and manage all assets and a representative general body (each constituency in the general body, either on the basis of ward or certain reserved categories, and women could have one representative for a general body) would also elect the Board of Directors and designate the powers that the Board of Directors and the Executive Committee would have to run the Society.

This Society would thus be governed by a professional Board of Directors including those elected by the shareholders. The Board will be assisted by an Advisory Body and specialized Sub-Committees consisting of experts from agriculture, allied activities and agro-industries. This Society, established at the village level itself, with full autonomy, would be governed by the vision, mission and objectives set out by the state level Advisory Council consisting of functional experts in animal husbandry, fisheries, sericulture, horticulture, retailing, rural industries, etc.

Every member of the Society should get no less than the best of the last five years' return at the beginning and would get multiples of it at the end of every year, proportionately distributed in accordance with their shareholding value. The Society should be run under Public Private Partnership (PPP) mode. The practical details of many of these aspects should find a place in a special law that can be formulated.

Roles and Responsibilities of Various Agencies are as follows:

1. State government should constitute a special Regulatory Authority to value and register the scrips.
2. In the event of the death of the actual owner evidenced by the Death Certificate, the legal heirs would get the shares as per the will, if any, of the deceased. And in its absence, the Society would retain the shares by transferring them in its own name and it should also be registered with the specified Authority. This would, in effect, enable all mutations recorded without having to sub-divide the land.

3. The Society should be registered with Articles and Memorandum of Association wherein the boundaries of functioning authorities and activities are clearly defined. If an existing PACS would like to perform these functions, it should be enabled through a transition clause in the proposed law.
4. The seed capital equivalent to the land value contributed by the farmers during the first five years should be mobilized at the rate of 10 percent of the value from the landowners. Those who lack liquidity at the start should be helped out by the National Farm Equity Fund to be specially set up with a corpus of Rs 5,000 crores initially, as a budgetary support.
5. Banks should sanction loans to the society on a debt equity ratio of 4:1 with a moratorium of two years on a soft rate of interest.
6. National Agricultural Insurance Corporation should insure agricultural loans.
7. General Insurance Corporation should insure the other assets in conjunction with the Life and Health Insurance of all the shareholders and the premium would be part of the project cost.
8. Initial project costs that include administrative and establishment expenses would be met out of the loan funds.
9. Existing liabilities to institutional lenders and other statutory agencies should be pooled into a separate liquid asset and blocked for a period of three years, interest frozen as on the date of transfer. This pooled asset in the financing bank's books would be a funded asset repayable after the moratorium period in seven instalments.
10. The state, as a one-time measure, may write off the private moneylenders' loans or de-recognize the usurious loans as part of the new law.
11. Lessee—whether oral or written—would have the scrip endorsed in favour of the lessee by the owner with attestation from the Society Management. All such recorded leases shall also be exempt from the fiduciary compulsions.
12. Each agricultural university and institutions like the National Academy of Agricultural Research Management (NAARM) should make the internship and research fellowships a compulsorily part of such projects for a period of six months, to help the society in project conceptualization.
13. NABARD field-level executives should render technical help in projectization and formulation of the village development plan.

14. NABARD should be asked to administer the National Farm Equity Fund.
15. NABARD should set up a district-level and state-level monitoring committee to oversee project implementation.
16. A Specified Authority should be provided with a list of chartered accountant firms to the Society at the village level for taking up half-yearly and annual audits. Each village Society should display its accounts in the Notice Board duly signed by the CA and Management representative.
17. In case natural calamities occur, and the village itself is washed out, the state government, after realizing insured amounts from the Insurance Companies, should re-carve the village and distribute the land in accordance with the share register so that the rehabilitated village carries on its economic activity undisturbed.
18. In the case of continuing natural calamities like cyclones, drought and periodical floods, insurance claims should be quickly settled in favour of the Society and the financing bank; the deficit should be financed by the state government and the bank from out of the Natural Calamity Fund to be separately set up by the Government of India with participation from the state government in equal proportion, and this fund would also be administered by the NABARD as the agent of Government of India.

Exit Route

1. Any member-farmer can sell his holding but should have the sale recorded and specifically approved by the Society. The sale should take place only through the Society as the proportional liability on the piece of land would be deducted by the Society at the point of materialization. The Contract for sale could be such that the buyer might pay in instalments, in which case, the first charge shall be of the Society and the final transfer of land would take place by means of Society recording in its share registry the new owner's name, after full consideration of sale is routed through the Society. The first preference for purchase shall be with the family members and in the absence of family members, the Society itself, and in case the price offered falls short of the outside buyer's offer, the latter would prevail subject to the buyer becoming a new member in the society.

2. At the end of every three years, the shares are revalued in terms of the annual dividend passed on at the general body. The share register would thus be updated in valuation terms, once every three years.

Other Aspects

Each member should be provided credit support for consumption and social needs as decided by the Board of Directors on such terms and conditions as considered appropriate and in the best interests of members.

The hinterland of the village should be enveloped by adequate and appropriate storage and marketing facilities as part of the project.

Integrated development of land-based and non-land-based activities, supporting and providing value addition to the farm produce right at the doorstep of the farmer through this new initiative, with appropriate laws would usher in an era of prosperity for not only farmers, but for the entire village.

All the Societies should be computerized from the very start and appropriate management information system should be designed by NABARD with the help of outside experts.

Caveats

The only problem is about insulating the entire system from political pollution. The whole concept would become effective when the following aspects are also considered as sine qua non of the project approach:

1. The indiscriminate land use change of agricultural lands to be curtailed.
2. The present day exorbitant input costs of agricultural operations by way of seeds, fertilizers, pesticides, etc, need to be brought down to minimize the risk aspect or at least regulate the supply system by way of issue of coupons in favour of the society, in sync with the cropping pattern adopted.

   Another way may be to gradually do away with the toxic chemical inputs without sacrificing production and productivity.
3. The post-harvesting systems to preserve the agricultural produce for longer periods. The multi-storied godowns and cold storage facilities should be set up in the market yard of the society so that the first leg of the commodity futures starts there.

4. The minimum returns are to be guaranteed on agricultural operations, by appropriate pricing of the agricultural produce, so as to make it attractive.
5. The serious constraint to sustain agricultural operations is non-availability of the required work force in the rural areas. This can be addressed adequately by integrating the MGNREGA with farm operations.

There must be a firm resolve that the governments would not indulge in loan write-off but would only facilitate financial unburdening through the specially set up funds. The whole scheme would thus help protect property rights without impeding economic development and legal disputes would also be minimized. All disputes should be settled through local arbitration mechanism.

[This is a modified version of the paper presented at the Symposium on Land Rights and Development, organized by the Liberty Institute, New Delhi, in association with Forum for Good Governance, Hyderabad on December 26, 2010.

I am thankful to M.S. Swaminathan for blessing the idea, Amit Barua, Director, Liberty Institute, New Delhi, and J. Rama Rao, activist, for the useful comments.]

FARM AND RURAL CREDIT ISSUES

CHAPTER 5

The Need for Imperatives of a Rural Credit Policy

A number of committees have gone into the institutional mechanisms, systems and procedures of rural credit during the past four decades, but there has been no attempt at laying down a specific policy for rural credit. A clear-cut approach towards the framing of a rural credit policy is urgently needed as rural credit markets today are at a cross-road, caught between the escapist approaches of the elitist bankers and the compulsive needs of the rural clientele. The demand for rural credit has been on the increase in the hitherto neglected areas like marketing support for rural industrial products; new technologies in the un-irrigated and semi-irrigated tracts; biotechnology; fisheries, commercial dairies, etc. However, there are several inadequacies and weaknesses in the existing framework for rural credit that has come to light in the course of implementation, which need to be addressed on an urgent basis. This chapter intends to examine the choice, adequacy, and appropriateness of both institutions and instruments of rural credit policy.

The Khusro Committee (1987) estimated, under four scenarios, the total volume of credit requirement for agriculture and rural development by the year 1994–95 at Rs 39,322 crore (Alternative 1), Rs 36,196 crore (Alternative 2), Rs 40,567 crore (Alternative 3) and Rs 49,582 crore (Alternative 4). Credit requirements for agriculture by the year 2000 were expected to increase from Rs 45,000 to Rs 60,000 crore (under Alternative 4). Considering these alternative projections, the total volume of credit flow for agriculture in 2009–10 stood at around Rs 3,84,514 crore.

Rural Credit Structure

Farm Credit Cooperatives (PACS) which have, no doubt, spread far and wide, have proved to be far too inadequate to the task of meeting the rural credit needs. The Cooperative Act has vested so much power with the Registrar of Cooperative Societies, as regards their functioning, that it has become very convenient for a politician to influence him for his own gains through these PACS. The politician-bureaucrat nexus has made the PACS non-economic entities and breeding grounds for politics in the villages. Democratic structures have not remained so, with elections to these bodies being held on political agenda and flags.

In the late 1960s and '70s, rural credit was identified with agricultural credit. The advent of the Green Revolution and infusion of new technologies called for widening and deepening of farm credit which necessitated the induction of commercial banks into the green fields. This period saw the birth of Agricultural Refinance Corporation (ARC) in 1966. (In 1974, this was re-christened as Agricultural Refinance and Development Corporation (ARDC), giving a "development" content to a refinancing function.)

The rural credit structure during this period suffered from the following weaknesses:

1. Cumbersome procedures leading to uneasy facilitation.
2. Political influence injected through nominees on the Boards of both commercial banks and Regional Rural Banks (RRBs).
3. Banks forsaking their role in appraisal systems by bowing down to the lists of beneficiaries and schemes handed down to them through the Block Development Officers and other government functionaries.
4. Gradual decline in recoveries.

Changes were then brought about through economic and financial sector reforms. With the capital adequacy norms introduced as a measure of financial sector reforms, the emphasis shifted to growth of income through non-interest sources. Rural credit through the banking system suffered enormously due to the above shift from rural development focus to income-growth focus. In fact, the government policies which were all along emphasizing cross-subsidization, parted ways.

Objectives of Rural Credit Policy

The objectives of rural credit policy should be in line with those of the overall plan objectives and should be subservient to the credit policy of the RBI. Among the major objectives of rural credit policy are the following:

1. To contribute to the growth impulses generated by the plan investments through properly supplementing the resources required for development of social and infrastructural sectors.
2. Creation of employment opportunities.
3. To promote entrepreneurial development in rural and semi-urban areas.
4. To strengthen the delivery systems to such a degree that the recycling of credit becomes an automatic process.
5. To impart a sense of seriousness in the deployment of credit for social structures through appropriate incentive mechanisms built into the lending system.
6. To ensure viability of the rural banking infrastructure by an appropriate restructuring and reorganization.
7. Market-driven interest rate structure even for agriculture and rural development with proper targeting of interest subsidization to the weaker sections of the community.

Status Report

RBI Act, 1934, enjoins upon it to "generally operate the currency and credit system of the country to its advantage." The predominance of agriculture in the country's economy was the natural setting for expanding and coordinating Agricultural Credit which is part of Rural Credit. Section 54 of the RBI Act lays down "Creation of a special Agricultural Credit Department" in the RBI "to study all aspects relating to Agricultural Credit and to coordinate RBI's relations with Cooperatives and banks engaged in the business of Agricultural Credit."[1]

The report of the All India Rural Credit Survey Committee (1954) which was accepted by the Government of India, state governments and RBI, contained important recommendations.

"State contribution to the share capital of Cooperative Credit Institutions and assigning to the RBI, a crucial role of implementing the scheme of integrated credit to build up a sound Cooperative Credit structure for providing timely credit to the Agricultural Sector."[2]

The Committee's recommendations also resulted in many innovative steps since taken for institution-building at all levels in the rural credit hierarchy, including the conversion of the Imperial Bank into the State Bank of India, the setting up of the National Cooperative Development Corporation (NCDC), and the creation of a wide network of Cooperative Training Institutions.

In July 1966, the Reserve Bank set up the All India Rural Credit Review Committee to undertake a comprehensive review of the recommendations of the Rural Credit Survey Committee, which resulted in assigning a dynamic role to the then ARC. This resulted in the adoption of various measures for ensuring timely and adequate flow of credit for agriculture through Cooperative and Commercial banks. The Multi-Agency approach was sought to be the remedy for strengthening the formal Rural Credit Markets. Commercial banks entered the sphere of Agricultural Credit on a massive scale after the nationalization of 14 public sector banks in 1969, followed by 6 more banks later. Further, with the establishment of the RRBs in 1975, one more wing was added to the Rural Credit Structure.[3]

The Multi-Agency approach no doubt resulted in the increased flow of credit through vigorous spread of the branches of both commercial banks and RRBs in the rural areas by deliberate strategy. In 1978, the RBI set up a Committee to Review Arrangements for Institutional Credit for Agricultural and Rural Development (CRAFICARD)—the third in the series of the studies the bank was undertaking in the field of rural credit. As a result of the recommendations of this committee, the Agricultural Credit Department from the RBI, which was handling refinance for the Cooperative Credit system, merged with ARDC to exclusively handle investment finance for agriculture, to form the NABARD in the year 1982.[4]

NABARD has emerged, therefore, as an apex central banking arm to evolve a rural credit policy consistent with national goals and create a climate conducive for achieving plan goals of the economy. While the institutional mechanisms have thus been strengthened to the present status, RBI introduced certain measures leading to planning of rural credit both at the grassroots and apex level.

A committee constituted by the RBI and headed by the former Deputy Governor P.D. Ojha, examined the system of rural credit planning and had recommended the introduction of Service Area approach or Command Area approach. Under this approach, each rural and semi-urban bank branch was supposed to prepare, after proper survey, village level credit plans for 15 to 25 villages coming under the command of each branch and aggregate them into a branch credit plan. The total sum of such bank credit plans combined with the estimated potential for agro-based projects in the urban sectors, would constitute the District Credit Plan (DCP). Every year, each rural and semi-urban bank branch is supposed to update the data and prepare the Annual Action Plans (AAP). Such planning, when synchronized with the bank's performance budget is expected to be grassroots level planning. Since April, 1989, Service Area Plans (SAP) came to be formulated. Simultaneously NABARD started preparing Potential Linked Plans (PLP) for each district, so the banking system could utilize these PLPs effectively in SAP targeting.

NABARD has been extending softer lines of refinance for investment credit, helping in farm planning, training manpower for handling rural development projects with care, extending technical assistance in a few cases, promoting entrepreneurial development, and facilitating forward integration in quite a few projects by appropriately liaising with state governments.

Institutional Credit

Institutional credit has certain special features when viewed as instrumental to rural development. First, it is not subject to budgetary uncertainties as the resources are largely drawn from the savings of the community by way of deposits. The quantum available at any point of time for rural development, then, becomes merely a matter of allocation policy. Secondly, as noted by CRAFICARD, institutional credit brings with it the experience and expertise of commercial banks, which are very relevant for rural development. Thirdly, it is expected to impose certain credit discipline, enforcing principle of recycling of credit and ensuring generation of incremental incomes for those who implement projects with full examination of techno-economic feasibility.

The Risk Spread

In 2001–02, 75 percent of credit flows have gone in favour of Punjab, Haryana, central and western Uttar Pradesh, Maharashtra and the 4 southern states. Likewise, nearly 70 percent of investment credit has been disbursed in the states of Punjab, Haryana, 4 southern states, Maharashtra, Madhya Pradesh and Uttar Pradesh. The credit-intensive areas are, therefore, mostly irrigation-intensive areas. Dryland agriculture, production of oil seeds and pulses received the least attention from commercial banks. The banks have, therefore, spread their credit net to areas where the risk is marginal.

Against this backdrop, it is worthwhile recalling what the committee on the Financial System (1991) had mentioned:

"The Committee believes that the issue is how to consolidate the quantitative gains that have been made while improving the quality of the loan portfolio and health of the banking system. Macro credit guidance should continue to be a legitimate aspect of development credit policy, but micro credit intervention, sometimes bordering on behest lending should be eschewed. Directed credit programmes have led to segmentation of credit markets and introduced an element of inflexibility in banking operations.... The growth of agriculture and small industry in India has now reached a point where legitimate productive requirements of these sectors (or large parts of them) could be met by banks on the basis of their commercial judgement."[5]

While the Committee's recommendations for reduction in the directed credit portfolio did not meet with the approval of the government, clubbing of direct and indirect categories of advances for agriculture within the sub-target of 18 percent for agriculture lending as a whole (subject to the stipulation that indirect lending should not exceed one-quarter of 18 percent), coupled with the decision to include advances granted up to Rs 5 lakhs for financing distribution of inputs for allied activities (such as cattle and poultry feed, etc) under indirect agricultural lendings, contributed effectively to reduction in the cake that could go to other perhaps less viable priority sectors. However, there can be no second opinion regarding the need for stepping up appraisal and supervisory skills in the management of rural credit and this would also call for specific policy interventions from the Central Banking institutions.

Social Banking on the Wane

The goal of nationalization of banks was to extend the reach of banking and financial services to all parts of the country and to all sections of society. During the first 10 years of bank nationalization, committee after committee was appointed to give a direction to banks in tune with the national social goals. Selective credit control regulations were modified from time to time to ration out credit to the areas which the government thought fit: 60 percent of credit-deposit ratio to be achieved in rural and semi-urban areas; 1 percent of the previous year's lendings to be earmarked for the depressed classes of society at differential rate of interest; 40 percent of the total volume of credit to be given to the priority sectors of which, agriculture was to receive 45 percent; small and marginal farmers were to receive due priority from the banks, etc. Refinance norms were simplified; security norms were relaxed. These policy interventions were duly supported by institutional mechanisms.

In recent years, we seem to have taken an about turn. The institutional mechanisms, so assiduously built up over the years, seem to be on their death bed despite a revamping measure introduced here and there. During the past few years, the slogans in the banking sector are merchant banking, lease finance, mutual funds, capital markets, etc. Forgotten are the objectives of bank nationalization.

However, the vastly spread formal credit markets, despite all their failings, have succeeded in influencing the terms of credit in informal credit markets, and thus helped the rural masses. The rates of interest in formal credit markets have come down from over 60 percent in 1969 to 9–12.25 percent (for loans less than 2 lakhs). But, with the banks dragging their feet since 1991, the informal credit markets have again been surging forward. This is demonstrated by the fact that, despite a decline in the percentage of credit for direct agriculture from commercial banks, agricultural production has not declined in recent years.

Notes

1. RBI Act, 1934.
2. B. Yerram Raju, 1954, All India Rural Credit Survey Committee, RBI.
3. B. Yerram Raju, 1978, Working Group on Regional Rural Banks, RBI.
4. B. Yerram Raju, 1982, Committee to Review Arrangements for Agriculture and Rural Development, RBI.
5. Narasimham Committee, 1991.

CHAPTER 6

Rural Banking: A Perspective for Development

In the post-nationalization era, there has been a significant change in the complexion of Indian banking, as evidenced by the following factors:

1. Banking has spread within easy reach of people. The total number of branches of commercial banks increased from 68,724 in June 2005 to 90,830 in June 2011. Out of these, 37.2 percent are located in rural areas. In terms of regional dispersal also, states which were less banked earlier, came to be better banked.
2. In the very important area of deposit mobilization, despite increasing competition from all quarters, including governmental agencies and other public sector undertakings, deposits grew from a mere Rs 4,665 crore in 1969 to Rs 5,39,314 crore as of December 2011.
3. There has been a substantial rise in investments of commercial banks in government securities to meet the requirements of statutory liquidity ratio.
4. Both the quantum and composition of advances underwent a significant change. There was a decline in the share of advances to large and medium industry, while credit to the priority sector increased significantly as a share of total advances of public sector banks.

Banking industry has acquired both strength and maturity, not only to mop up national savings but also to meet credit expectations of traditional and new sectors. Thus, it has emerged as a potent instrument to execute the Plan objectives.

As a result of the change in approach to rural banking, three distinct characteristics have emerged:

1. The use of banks' resources in some areas which were considered budgetary responsibilities of the state/central governments. A plethora of institutions like the Irrigation Development Corporation, Land Development Corporation, etc, were created by almost all the state governments with their own seed capital. Matching resources to meet the special goals were raised through the banking industry. As a result of low investment/output ratio, apart from the failure of these organizations to meet the objectives for which they were set up, substantial resources of the commercial banks are blocked. No doubt, several state governments which sought financial assistance for these Corporations gave their guarantees to the banks. The government guarantees, by themselves, do not signify anything unless the Corporations are enabled to contribute to the desired extent to national development and growth, by working in an efficient manner and generating surpluses to meet the debt commitments.
2. Increased use of banks' funds for stepping up production in agricultural and allied sectors, handloom, village and cottage industries, etc, through direct assistance to the beneficiaries. In the case of agriculture, the size of the farm unit is a formidable constraint to formulate viable investment programmes. Notwithstanding the phenomenal rise in credit and farm output, if banks are asked to continue funding this activity without the necessary infrastructural and administrative support, it may not be possible for banks to sustain the burden of default, losses and other costs. For a variety of reasons, including beneficiary's lack of awareness, defective scheme formulation and absence of education of the beneficiary, there were poor recoveries, particularly in agriculture and allied sectors. Year after year, the overdues that are mounting are a cause of great concern. Unless banks' resources are appropriately recycled to cover more and more target groups year after year, economic development through credit delivery mechanism would not be possible.
3. Participation of the banking industry in anti-poverty programmes. Delayed decisions on certain aspects having policy implications, untimely flow of credit, and under-financing have also been responsible for ineffective implementation of various anti-poverty programmes so

far. In fact, to a certain extent, these factors are also responsible for poor recoveries or repayments. Further, commitment on the part of the ground level functionaries to the task of rural development and adequate administrative back-up of the banks also become necessary concomitants of this process.

Today, the banking system in the country is better equipped than before to promote rural development. The objectives would be better achieved only when proper coordination exists among the sponsoring agencies, technical experts and the banking institutions.

Giving Due Credit to Farm Credit: Need of the Hour

Credit for agriculture from the commercial banking system has been on the decline during the past 10 years. But food production has been on the increase. Stocks have been bulging in the food godowns. There was also a white revolution. Production of fruits and vegetables has also increased considerably during this period. This does not mean that agricultural production is independent of credit. On the other hand, credit for agriculture is essential for the simple reason that the farmer's production is locked up either in land or stock at a time when he requires cash for investment. It simply means that the farmer is forced to meet his cash requirements from private moneylenders at usurious interest rates. The growing suicides of farmers reported in recent years are a reflection of the failure of the organizational lending system. The number of accounts is continuously on the decline if we are to go by the reports of the Trend and Progress of Banking in India published by the RBI.

"It is in the context of the massive credit requirements for successful implementation of the new agricultural strategy and the inability of the cooperatives alone to meet the demand, that the Multi-Agency Approach has come to be aaccepted."[1]

It would be interesting to note that the number of direct agriculture accounts declined from 20.7mn in 1995 to 18.7mn in 1998 but later increased to 40.6mn by June 2012, with the annual targets of short-term lending set in the Central Budgets by the Finance Minister for the public sector banks. The outstanding short-term direct agricultural credit shot up to Rs 46,10,229 mn by June 2012. (Outstanding Credit includes unpaid interest and miscellaneous expenses and not net disbursements. However, ever since the reclassification of assets came into being as a consequence of reforms in the banking sector, the outstandings do not include more than two quarters of unpaid interest up to 1996–97 and 4 quarters or 2 harvest seasons thereafter.)

Financing Crop Loans for Leaseholders

In the case of sharecroppers, who form a special category and who do not have any recorded rights in land, banks would be able to grant loans only if their status is properly recorded in the record of land rights. Further, they should be enabled to create a charge on the crops raised by them, notwithstanding the fact that they are not the owners of the land over which the crop is raised by them.

Early instructions regarding loans to sharecroppers are still in vogue but not under actual implementation

Those farmers who own some land and also cultivate some land as tenants or sharecroppers may be assisted for crop loan both on the owned land and the land held under tenancy.

Further, those sharecroppers who do not own any land can be granted crop loans subject to ensuring the following:

1. The bank should be satisfied about the existence of tenancy and be in a position to identify the plot of land under cultivation by the tenant.
2. The applicants should be vested, by suitable legislation, with rights to create a charge on the crops raised by them (to the extent of their interest in the land) to secure financial assistance from the bank, notwithstanding the fact that they are not the owners of the land on and from which the crop is raised.
3. The borrower should, in each case, furnish to the bank satisfactory evidence to the effect that he is actually engaged in the cultivation of land, which bears a specific survey number.
4. Loans can be sanctioned on group guarantee basis and the bank should not take any responsibility to form groups.

Loans under Tie-up Arrangements

Banks can sanction loans to farmers under tie-up arrangements with the traders or manufacturers, with a few advantages:

1. Guarantees can be obtained for repayment of the loans from the agencies concerned.

2. There is no need to be confined to village adoption/service area approach.
3. Inspections can be carried out by the field staff only on 10 percent random sample to satisfy that the amount lent is actually used for that purpose.
4. The banks should analyse the balance sheets of the link agencies and compile opinion reports on them to ensure that the agencies are good for the liability.

Note

1. R.K. Talwar, 1970, 'Expert Group on State Enactments', Ch. 7, p. 31.

CHAPTER 7

Investment Credit in Agriculture

Availability of banking institutions within an easy reach of farmers, infrastructural framework for supporting agricultural operations, the spurt in the number of sponsoring agencies, etc, have contributed to farmers' reliance on institutional credit for long-term operations on an increasing scale in the recent years. Credit for investment purposes is provided by commercial banks in the shape of agricultural term loans. It results in creation of capital asset capable of generating/increasing productivity and production over period of time. The basic difference between a short- and medium-term loan is that while repayment in respect of the former comes from regular farm accruals, in respect of the latter, it comes from incremental returns, generated from the utilization of the asset(s) acquired. The purposes for which these agricultural term loans are granted, can be broadly classified as follows:

1. On-farm investments like development of land per se, systematic land development under command areas; minor irrigation of all types (dug wells, dug-cum-bore wells, bore wells, shallow tube wells, lift irrigation schemes, energization of all these investments either through electric or diesel power) soil conservation, etc.
2. Farm mechanization like power-sprayers, winnowers, threshers, power-tillers, tractors, harvester-combines, etc.
3. Diversified purposes like horticulture, sericulture, apiculture (bee keeping), inland and marine fisheries, social and farm forestry, dairy, poultry, sheep and goat-rearing, piggery, etc.
4. Marketing and storage like storage godowns, market yards, silos, etc.

It is necessary that the aforementioned schemes/proposals should be economically viable for a banker to support. This would mean that the project should be in a position to repay its cost (not loan component alone) well within the life of the asset, with interest out of the net incremental surplus accruing to the farmer from such a project. The scheme/project should necessarily be technically feasible (details of these will be adumbrated in the following pages).

More often than not, economic viability of an agricultural project is difficult to be determined. Careful assessment of what constitutes the cost of the components of a project, and the return on the project, has to be done.

Every term loan proposal requires an independent appraisal as each farmer is independent of the other and each farmer's peculiarities and environment have a significant contribution to make for his investment proposition to be fruitful. It would, in the usual course, entail the following steps:

1. During the pre-sancted visit, the banker should scan the environment and infrastructure available, examine the tenure, and assess the need for the investment proposed by the farmer, and ability of the farmer to maintain the asset during its productive life.
2. Interview the farmer about the pre-investment level of operations and income and collect the loan application form.
3. Collect the supporting documents of title like land records (10–1, 10–2 or Khasra Pahani or Pahani Patrika or an Agricultural Pattadar Passbook under the state's record of the Rights Act), where necessary from other lending institutions, particularly the government and the cooperatives, to avoid concurrent borrowings, etc. It is, however, necessary to ensure that the farmer is neither harassed nor compelled to run to various places for securing this supporting information. In case there are large numbers of applicants for similar investments and from a compact area, arrangements should be made by the lending institution to procure required reports by coordinating with the agencies concerned.
4. Verify information relating to costs of investment and prices with reference to the market prices of outputs and farm-gate prices for outputs.
5. Determine the seasonality and sanction the advance prescribing the necessary terms and conditions with the specific knowledge and understanding of the farmer.

6. Complete documentation of the loan, mentioning therein the schedule of disbursement and schedule of repayment.
7. Disburse loan amount as per schedule. Sometimes rigidly following the schedule may harm the investment pattern. The officer should be circumspect and ensure that the investment materializes as programmed and comes into productive use before the season. This would call for close supervision and follow-up.

   There are common complaints of banks' non-cooperative attitude in the matter of disbursement of loans. Care should be taken that while an unscrupulous applicant is not allowed to inflate prices of assets to be acquired/investments to be made, the genuine needs of other applicants should be met in a timely and adequate manner. An inflexible/conservative approach may at times reduce the rate of return on the investments proposed to be made.
8. Post-disbursement and follow-up.

   Thus, knowledge of the area where investment is proposed and beneficial is crucial to ensure success of any farm investment proposal.

   Although every farm investment has its specificities considering the individual farmer's requirements, the viability of the proposal does not rest on such individual farmer's environs. Viability necessarily depends on the forward and backward linkages. The backward linkages rest on the supply of inputs of adequate quantity and appropriate quality, at reasonable prices. Likewise, the forward linkages rest on storage, marketing, etc. While in the case of large and medium farmers, access to these linkages does not pose a problem. In the case of small farmers, their access has to be ensured by the lending agency through appropriate planning, programming, involvement and coordination with various agencies that are responsible for their provision.

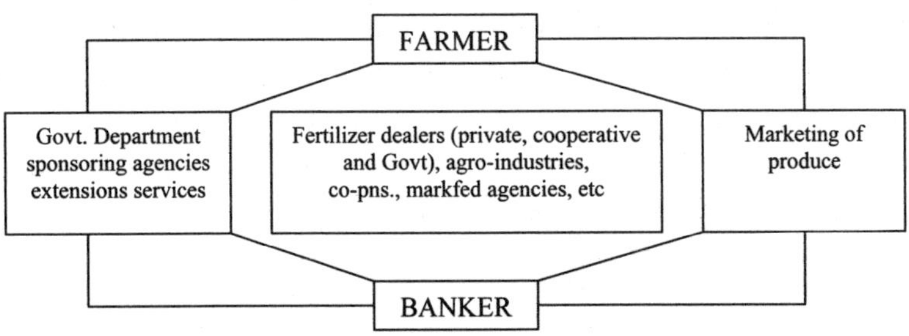

The farmer's relationship with either government department, for purposes of identification or extension, or with input supply agencies and marketing agencies is a one-sided affair, whereas with the banker, it is two-sided. The banker has a responsibility to not merely ensure disbursal of money for creation of an asset and maintaining it in productive use during its lifetime, but also to get back the amount advanced. The relationship between the banker and farmer should necessarily be cyclical, inter-dependent and one that would sustain confidence in each other. The dependence co-efficiency among small farmers in this framework is so high that the banker should adopt an approach or strategy different from the others. It is in such a context that the banker should resort to preparation of area development schemes on project basis. Preparation of area development schemes involves a little expertise on the part of the lender. The lending banker has to decide an area which is compact and capable of easy supervision and monitoring of investments on an on-going basis. If this area is served only by one bank branch, that branch can formulate the scheme and seek approval of the controlling authority. If, on the other hand, the area is served by more than one branch of a single bank and has potentials for large investments of an identical nature, all the branches of this bank and the scheme formulation involving these many branches can be done by the controlling authority itself. The project formulation approach to investment credit has assumed greater importance, with the erstwhile ARDC (NABARD) providing refinance to the primary lending banks on a schematic basis since the beginning of 1970s. When the significance and advantages of project approach/schematic lendings were realized by NABARD, even the World Bank credit on soft terms was made available to the country. The guidelines for project formulation, which are discussed in the following pages, are therefore based on the principles dictated by the World Bank.

The size of operations in agricultural investment credit and the complexities are as high and varied as to necessitate the commercial banking system to place its reliance on NABARD in an increasing measure year, after year. NABARD, in the process, tried to bring about uniformity among the various participating agencies which include cooperatives also, over the unit costs, appraisal systems, monitoring and evaluation techniques. The NABARD circularized among the participating institutions scheme-wise guidelines, which are given in the annexure to this chapter.

Project Approach to Investment Credit and Project Management

To quote J. Price Gittinger, the renowned World Bank Economist: "Projects are the cutting edge of development"[1]. The whole complex of activities involved in using resources to gain benefits constitutes our "project". "It is an activity which logically lends itself to planning, financing and implementing as a unit. It is a specific starting unit and a specific ending point. It is something which is meaningful both in its major costs and returns. It is a proposal for capital investment to develop facilities for providing goods and/or services. It is not so easy to define a project as to work it out in practice."

As it has been seen earlier, the purpose of financing agriculture is not just to replace individual moneylenders but to enable agriculture and the former to move on to a higher level of technology that would create substantial basis for increase in agricultural output, to increase the number of mandays of employment and to have much better indicators of development in terms of productivity, both of land and of human beings. This calls for an integrated approach. If, instead of a particular investment, the area as a whole is proposed to be developed, a single project would not be adequate. A related set of projects may envisage simultaneous development of land, irrigation, cattle breeding and upgradation, storage and marketing facilities, roads, processing facilities and sometimes educational and medical care, etc, along with economic growth, if it is intended to improve the quality of life in the project area. Quite rightly, the whole complex of these and similar measures is usually considered together, as many of them, in isolation and without the others, would be of little use. A "package" approach is required right from the stage of formulation itself. The pattern of inter-related systems of development measures are not completely rigid. The sub-projects and alternative patterns of investment need to be considered, if agricultural development projects are not to be wrongly rejected or too readily accepted. A cyclical relationship exists in project management from the starting point to the ending point.

PROJECT CYCLE

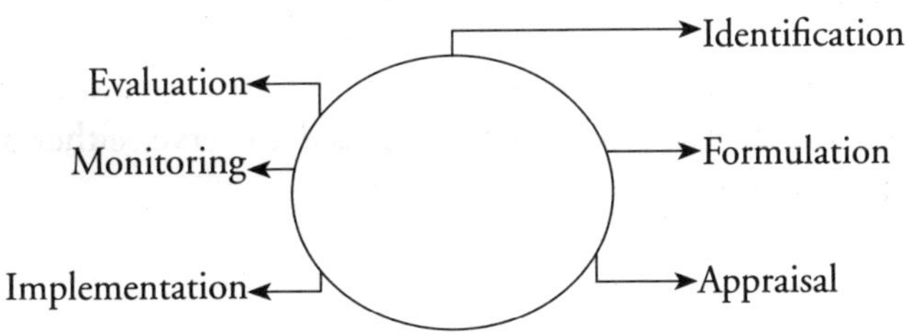

Experience shows, especially in agriculture, that, "If planning efforts were redirected towards effecting improvements in more critical areas of project planning, considerable improvement in project performance could result in benefits to the investor. The project plan consists of many components in an interdependent system. There is considerable uncertainty about each element, particularly in an agricultural project. Irrespective of the theoretical deficiencies of appraisal, project performance will be critically affected by the accuracy of the forecast demands, prices, costs, returns, management and so on. These factors are an integral part of the project plan."[2]

Identification

Identification of the area of the project is the first and foremost step in project management. This would depend on the following considerations:

1. The need for the project in the area.
2. Availability of inputs required in project implementation.
3. Backwardness of the area.
4. The extent to which the project would subserve the overall national goals.
5. The extent to which regional imbalances could be set right.
6. The benefits that would accrue to the farming community and the area as a whole, etc.

In theory, the identification, selection and preparation of projects should follow from an overall national development plan, which will have identified the priority sectors and production targets, thereby providing the criteria for the selection of projects. In practice, they are usually selected to meet identified specific needs or to take advantage of special opportunities—the presence of natural resources or some other special circumstances permitting production of a commodity at a relatively low cost, or a potential for exports, and so on.

Detailed Survey

A detailed socio-economic survey of the project area should be conducted. Depending on the area the project is supposed to serve, either a census or sample should be designed.

Costs, Size of Holding and Target Farm Income

The project area may not always be compact, and the target group may not also be uniform in terms of the assets held. Therefore, determining project costs becomes crucial. The investment may vary within the project area itself. Taking these variations into account, realistic estimates will have to be prepared by competent technical staff. In order to arrive at the average unit costs, the varying costs of units in different area should be the basis. Usually, NABARD provides this unit cost for all eligible farm investments on regional basis. It is not as though these unit costs are permanent. They need not be stable even during the project period. A State Level Committee on unit costs consisting of representatives of lead banks, the NABARD and state level technical functionaries, meets once in six months to prescribe these unit costs when the recommendations from the various districts are also examined. Variations to the extent of 10 percent are generally permitted even without reference to NABARD, provided the overall project costs do not show an increase in the aggregate. A 20 percent increase in unit costs can be affected by the NABARD's regional office on the recommendation of State Level Committee on unit costs. Beyond this, the matter will have to be referred to NABARD's central office at Bombay.

"On any farm development project, the smaller the prescribed size of holding, the greater the number of holdings and settler families, and therefore, the employment impact. The greater the number of settler families, the lower the total project costs per family; also given the farming system, the farm income per holding and per farm family will be lower. The project approach is commonly criticized because of the limited impact on the rural poor in terms of employment and incomes."[3]

Financial Resources

The level of rise in income would depend upon the weight age given to various project objectives. Lower project costs per settler are achieved by planning for smaller holdings and therefore, more settlers, when the object is to take care of problems of poverty and increased employment. Such a project might not envisage a large rise in production, which, of course, can be tackled by taking up other types of projects.

The criterion used by the World Bank agricultural project planners is the "target farm income". Farm income is the product of the farming system and the size of holding, so that given the farming system, the "optimum size of the holding will be determined by the level of target farm income."[4] This is invariably achieved through preparation of a few farm models under farm budgeting.

Sufficient care has to be taken while selecting farm models; particular attention is required to be paid to the following, among other things:

1. Different models might involve different unit sizes; care may be exercised to ensure that they are optimum and economical units under the given circumstances.
2. Hydrogeological, geophysical and other technical aspects concerning the units should be carefully studied before choosing representative units.
3. In case of land-based units, one has to examine the cropping pattern. Farmers being responsive to price of inputs and outputs, cost-intensive or high risk bearing crops in the "with" project situation, may not find ready acceptance. A gradual switch over and the consequent low returns in the initial years of project implementation form a very important factor in farm models.
4. In the case of minor irrigation schemes, only the benefiting area or the command area of the well should be taken into consideration under a representative unit. Though the farmer may own a larger holding, only a fraction of it might receive benefit of irrigation from the new investment; only the command area should be taken into account.

Financial Resources

The financial resources for the project must be commented upon. The successful implementation of the project would depend upon the timely availability of the required investment as per projections. It is not enough if adequacy of long-term or capital resources is ensured. The success of the project would depend upon the ready availability of short-term or working capital resources in adequate measure, either through institutional or individual sources.

What is true of the World Bank's approach to project lending is equally true for a commercial bank's approach in this area. The bank's approach has taught them that in project appraisal nothing should be taken for granted and that healthy scepticism is a cardinal virtue. This scepticism must be applied to the economic, technical, institutional and financial aspects of the project appraisal, beginning with a questioning of the basic statistical data to make sure that a false sense of accuracy has not been imparted through the application of sophisticated techniques of analysis to questionable basic data.

The appraisal of a proposed project from an economic point of view represents an attempt to answer these questions: (a) is the project in a sector of development, which is likely to contribute significantly to the development of the whole economy? (b) is the project likely to contribute effectively to the development of that sector and; (c) is the contribution likely to justify the use of the quantity of scarce resources namely, capital, managerial talent, skilled labour, etc., that are available.

The starting point of the analysis is to specify all the expected inputs and outputs of the project and to put a price to each such input and output. In this way, one arrives at anticipated expenditures and receipts. These will be spaced over time, from the inception of planning to the economic demise of the project (that is, when it ceases to be profitable to operate it), or to eternity. These estimates are then combined into some measure of profitability.

For purposes of prognosis and for assessing the reliability of such forecast, all the values of the receipts from the project and the expenditure on the project during its lifetime should, wherever possible, be split into quantities and prices. To ensure that all related receipts and expenditures are taken into account, the total effect of the project upon the area must be considered. A social cost-benefit analysis may revalue the quantities of goods and services used and produced (that is, profitability).

The reliability of the basic figures—the quantities and prices of inputs and outputs—depends upon three kinds of considerations:

1. Technical.
2. Human and managerial.
3. Economic.

Technical feasibility would depend on the agro-climatic situation, resource availability and utilization, mechanization of the processes involved and other infrastructure available. The beneficiaries should be in a position to absorb the credit in the required direction and must be prepared to accept the technological advancement necessary for quicker implementation and enlargement of benefits from the projects. Lack of or inadequacy of management and skills is more often the cause for disappointment in the implementation of the project. It has been our experience that many projects take a longer time than envisaged in the original report for full implementation. The reasons could be manifold. Input costs escalation might not have been adequately accounted for; there might not have been proper coordination between the various agencies involved in project implementation; or there has been such a vast change in the agro-climatic conditions that it would no longer be useful to take up the project in the interregnum between project formulation and sanction; or that another government agency may have preponed its investment due to political pressures which may necessitate a change in the project, and so on.

Coming to the economic assumption which lies behind the basic figures used for the economic evaluation of profitability or cost-benefit analysis, it is necessary to fix specific price to each unit of output following form the project during its life time (shadow prices). Actual base prices must be applied to the various inputs in the project. There are three measures used to assess project worth:

Benefit cost ratio:	Present worth of benefits / Present worth of costs
Net present worth (NPW):	Present worth of benefits minus present worth of costs
Internal rate of return (IRR):	The interest rate at which the present worth of benefits equals the present worth of costs of the project

Where, i=IRR, I=net investment in each year
B=net benefits in each year
0,1,2…….n=represents years starting from the present

$$IO + I \left[\frac{I}{(1+i)}\right] + I_2 \left[\frac{I+}{(1+i)^2}\right]$$

$$BO + BI \left[\frac{I}{(1+i)}\right] + B_2 \left[\frac{I+B_n}{(1+i)^2}\right] \left[\frac{1}{(1+i)^n}\right]$$

Whenever the benefit cost ratio is 1 or more than 1, it indicates that the project is financially profitable. Similarly, NPW gives the present value of the surplus of benefits that the project will generate, over and above what will be available if the amount proposed to be invested in the project is invested at the current rate of interest elsewhere (opportunity cost). IRR on the other hand, enables us to select from among several projects that is, rank them. IRR does not depend on the market rate of interest. It only reflects the interest that the project can bear. Therefore, the higher the IRR compared to market rate of interest, the more attractive is the project.

This economic analysis is, therefore, necessary to ensure that the total return or productivity or profitability to the whole society or whole economy comes up as expected and that all the resources committed to the project, regardless as to who in the society contribute to them, are economically used.

In contrast, the individual financial entities—the farmers, artisans, and small industrialists or other small businessmen—each is properly concerned about the return to the equity he contributes. This is ensured by financial analysis. Since the benefits of integrated area development are essentially expected to reach the economically backward/weaker sections of the community, the equity capital contribution of these sections is subsidized by the government itself. Therefore, in integrated area small development projects, economic analysis is more important than financial analysis. In view of the urgency with which these projects need to be formulated and appraised, the more sophisticated systems of DCF and IRR may not be of so much relevance as basing them on cost-benefit ratios.

It is, therefore, important to make a clear distinction between the economic appraisal of a project on the one hand and the appraisal of its financial consequences on the other. The two types of appraisal are directed at different questions and require a different measure of costs and benefits. The economic appraisal is concerned with the real economic costs and benefits of the project and with the problem of allocating resources so as to maximize the benefits for the country as a whole. The financial appraisal considers the costs and benefits of a project in terms of actual receipts and expenditures only, in order to assess the self liquidating character of the project, the adequacy of its incentives, and its impact on government funds.

Project Management

Having said so much about the economic analysis and appraisal of a project, it is necessary to highlight certain important and relevant factors about project management.

Every lending institution will have to devote its attention to project management in an adequate measure, in order that the project benefits reach the intended beneficiaries to the desired extent. This involves timely monitoring of the project. Project formulation, sanction and disbursement of loans constitutes only the first half of the development programme; the second half of the task is to keep track of what happens to the loan amount and the loanees so as to ensure that: (a) the loan is not misused, and; (b) the loanee derives the maximum benefit from the investment. It is essential to have feedback to learn about operational and other deficiencies to enable the bank to take timely corrective action. To improve the quality and accuracy of the project work and to speed up project implementation, the feedback data from the field level is also necessary to provide the base for future project formulations.

The post-loan disbursement is a three-dimensional task involving: (a) the information collection system; (b) short-term studies focusing their attention on:

(i) Whether investment is proceeding as envisaged.
(ii) Whether physical and financial targets are being achieved as per programme.
(iii) Whether the loan is being effectively supervised.
(iv) Whether terms and conditions stipulated at the time of sanction are being adhered to; and

(c) long-term studies for evaluation of economic benefits—to evaluate the validity of various assumptions made (additional irrigated area, cropping pattern, crop intensity, net incremental income, in respect of agricultural investments; increase in milk yield, dairy products and the change in the breed over the years, etc in respect of dairy farms, etc.). If monitoring studies are not periodically conducted to highlight the deficiencies and to benefit from the experiences of the past by the project implementing agencies in a systematic manner, there is a danger of these investments ending up as academic exercises.

Project Evaluation

In regard to completed schemes, an assessment of their financial and economic development programme and for future project preparation. Such assessment has to include: (a) an analysis of the factors affecting the overall performance of the scheme, and; (b) a comparison between pre-investment assumptions and post-investment achievements. If there is any divergence between assumptions and achievements, causative factors that should have come to light in the monitoring studies should be thoroughly analysed and duly rectified. Finally, one would also like to know the specific aspects connected with (a) investment itself, and; (b) other factors essential for the investment to yield maximum benefits.

Logically, the evaluation has to centre round the farmer because that is the level where the final benefit is realized and also the level above which the data does not flow through the normal management information system. With the farmer at the centre of the evaluation study, data on farm business and farmer's backward and forward linkages have to be obtained. The data should be collected through specifically designed cultivator schedules. Backward linkages are those that would indicate the relationship of the borrower with the lending agencies, extension and supply agencies, etc. Forward linkages relate to the price available for the produce, marketing facilities, etc. Then farm level position (quality of project work, a sort of a technical evaluation, project costs, time-lag in investment completion and cause of delay if any, project utilization, etc.) will have to be evaluated. As in case of follow-up or monitoring studies, evaluation studies also call for specification of priorities. The priorities may obviously lie in the direction of obtaining the grass-root level picture of different types of schemes in different areas within as short a period as possible.

In fact, a project approach for integrated area development is essential to realize the benefits of development in a systematic manner. Every project must be appraised properly in order that the benefits of the project percolate to the entire area and not merely to a few individual beneficiaries. Economic analysis of the project, based on cost-benefit ratios with the help of shadow prices, should be carried out. Every lending institution should carry out monitoring studies at regular periodical intervals as part of project management and ensure that the deficiencies in one project are not repeated in future projects.

While project approach would ensure proper percolation of benefits to the target groups, it does not discount the need for examination of some important aspects like security, margins and repayment capacity.

Security

All land-based investments and investments seeking collateral securities (bearing in mind the overall relaxations granted to the weaker sections) require verification of certain documents vis-à-vis the statements made by the beneficiary in his application, like *jamabandi, girdawari* title deeds, etc. In a project where it is assumed that the individual loans would be secured by a charge on land, it is desirable to get the documents verified by a person having knowledge in this area, in order to ensure that the property offered as security to the bank conveys a clear, marketable and unencumbered title, and is within the ceiling and other laws enacted by the respective state government. If consolidation of holdings is in operation, it is desirable to avoid taking mortgage as security.

Margin

Banks often insist on the contribution of the beneficiary in the investment activity. This margin is provided (a) to ensure that the borrower evinces keen interest in the activity because of his stake; (b) to cover the risk arising from fluctuations in prices of securities offered to the bank. In agricultural activities, it may not be wise to insist on margins unless the viability, for lack of it, is going to be affected. The reason is that agriculturist's capital is locked up in land and stock. The maximum margin that can be expected could be 25 percent of the cost of investment.

The NABARD has prescribed the margins as follows:

Small farmers (whose annual income from the farm is below Rs 4,300): 5 percent. Even if more than one small farmer is involved, under joint or group investments, only this margin is expected. In case a sponsoring agency promotes the investment, the subsidy or margin money granted by it can be taken as his stake in the venture.

Medium farmers: 10 percent. In the case of joint or group investments, this can be reduced to 7.5 percent.

Large farmers: 15 percent. In the case of joint or group investments this can be reduced to 10 percent.

Repaying capacity

This should be judged on the basis of net incremental returns arising out of the investment proper. What is critical is fixation of appropriate gestation period. In several land based schemes like minor irrigation and land development, it will take a minimum period of two years for the benefits of the scheme to percolate. Immediately after development, the farmer will not adopt the cropping pattern that would absorb the changes introduced. This is particularly so in the case of small and marginal farmers in whose case, even after benefits accrue from the investments, the demands for consumption on incremental incomes will be high. It should, therefore, be realized that (a) incremental incomes will not be generated immediately after the capital investment is made on land, and; (b) even after incremental incomes are generated, it is wrong to assume that much of it would be available for either repayment or plough-back. Hence a suitable gestation period and long repayment period within the life of the project is worthwhile.

It should also be borne in mind that interest should not be compounded for the farming community as per the RBI's directives. The directives are that interest should be applied only when principal is due. If the principal is not paid on due date, consequent on application of interest on the due date, it gets compounded. If interest is applied at half-yearly or quarterly intervals, when the farmer does not have any liquidity to answer the demand, it will not be possible for the farmer to repay, and interest applied is likely to turn out as penalty on the farmer.

Appraisal of a few of the schemes should serve as models. The costs and returns mentioned therein should be subject to change depending on the area of the project and the prices of various inputs prevailing at the material time of appraisal.

1. Land development
2. Minor irrigation

   Dug well with pump set | Tube well | Electric pump set

3. Financing of tractor
4. Financing of dairy
5. Financing of poultry scheme
6. Financing of grape cultivation
7. Financing of orchards
8. Financing of gobar gas plant
9. Financing of tea plantation

10. Financing of sheep-rearing
11. Financing of marine fisheries
12. Financing of inland fisheries (pond cultivation)

Checklists for the bankers to finance them have been provided by NABARD.

Notes

1. J. Price, Gittinger, *Economic Analysis of Agricultural Projects*, Bombay, A World Bank Publications, reprinted by ARDC, p. 1.
2. Eric Clayton, 1983, *Agriculture, Poverty & Freedom in Developing Countries*, Macmillan Publications, p. 185.
3. Eric Clayton, ibid, p. 187.
4. Eric Clayton, 1975, *Agricultural Employment Creation and Small Holder,Rubber Production in Sumatra: Issue 2 of Occasional Paper*, Wye College, Agrarian development Unit.

Reference

B. Yerram Raju, 1992, "Project Sustainability in Indian Agriculture", *Prashasan Journal*, Rajasthan Institute of Public Administration.

CHAPTER 8

National Bank for Agriculture and Rural Development (NABARD)

ARC was created in July 1963 to oversee the medium- and long-term credit of the cooperative sector initially, as it was felt that the RBI was unable to cope with the requirements of the agricultural sector in terms of long- and medium-term credit. It was also felt that an independent organization would perhaps be necessary to give confidence to external funding agencies to invest capital in Indian agriculture and channel it through one conduit which could ensure proper supervision and follow-up of those funds disbursed through a multitude of primary units. The ARC started serving as an extended arm of the RBI ever since its inception, overseeing the disbursement of medium- and long-term credit disbursed through the land mortgage/ land development/ agricultural development banks in the cooperative sector. There, agencies used to be funded through flotation of debentures adequate enough to meet with the lending requirements of those banks in each year, which were being supported by the state governments.

Since the nationalization of commercial banks in 1969, the ARC was to play a more active role. The earlier security- oriented approach of the ARC was also to undergo a change in line with the change in the general climate of lending systems in the country. The systems of ARC that suited providing finance to cooperative term lending agencies, needed required a change to meet the requirements of commercial banks. Yet, as a funding agency at the national level, it could not draw a distinction between its different participating institutions. It strived to bring about uniformity in lending norms and systems between the various participating institutions. It has also lined up a credit channel from the World Bank and strengthened the training mechanism through the various regional training centres established at the land development/ agricultural development banks and its own College of Agricultural Banking in Pune.

The Agricultural Credit Department of the RBI continues to look after the short-term credit of the agricultural sector in the cooperative system. Short-term credit, at no point of time, has been inhibited by the requirements of monetary policy, as the RBI has always accorded a preferential treatment to rural credit and has imposed only such minimum operational disciplines as are necessary to ensure the sound health of the cooperative credit structure.

Responding to the emerging needs of the banking sector, the ARC reformed itself into the ARDC in 1975, to emphasize its developmental role. All the State Cooperative Banks, State Land Development Banks (SLDB) and the commercial banks have become shareholders of the ARDC. The apex structure by the beginning of 1980 could be summarized as in the following table:

Institution	*Periodicity of credit*	*Control*
1. Cooperative Societies at primary level through the DCCBs and State Cooperative Banks	Short- and Medium-Term Credit	Agricultural Credit Department of the RBI
2. Cooperative Land Development Banks or Land Mortgage Banks or Cooperative Agriculture Development Banks	Medium- and Long-Term Credit	Agricultural Credit Department of the RBI and the ARDC
3. Commercial Banks	Medium- and Long-Term Credit	DBOD, RBI and ARDC
4. Regional Rural Banks	Short-, Medium- and Long-Term Credit	DBOD, RBI and ARDC

The committee on Multi-Agency Approach to Institutional Credit for Agriculture estimated the credit requirements of the agricultural sector as at the end of March 1985 at Rs 16,480 crores. But the CRAFICARD arrived at an estimate of Rs 9,400 crores by about the same period, which was precisely the order estimated by the National Commission on Agriculture. It has been realized that the requirements of agriculture and rural development and the complications in multi-agency credit institutional system warrant an independent apex policy making body. It is in this background that the CRAFICARD has set aside the earlier views on the creation of an all-India institution for credit dispensation for agriculture, which mentioned that such an all-India institution will only add to the costs of credit and red tape associated with its procedures without adding to the resources or efficiency of the system or service to the cultivator.[1] Even the Administrative Reforms Commission (1970) did not favour the creation of a separate institution. But the National Commission on Agriculture (1976) favoured the creation of an all-India Institution—the Agricultural Development Bank of India. With the turn of the decade, the CRAFICARD felt that the time was opportune for a major structural change at the apex level and recommended the creation of NABARD, which was supposed to give undivided attention to providing all kinds of production and investment credit to agriculture, tiny sector, artisans, village and cottage industries, handicrafts and other allied activities in an integrated manner.

The NABARD Bill was passed by the Parliament on December 1, 1981. It came into existence on July 12, 1982 and started functioning with effect from July 15, 1982. NABARD has taken over the entire undertaking and business of ARDC, the refinancing functions of the RBI in relation to the State Cooperative Banks and RRBs. All the functions of the Agricultural Credit Department of the RBI, which include the management of long-term operation fund and long-term stabilization fund, were also taken over by NABARD. The authorized share capital of the bank is Rs 500 crores whereas paid-up capital is Rs 100 crores. Paid-up capital is contributed by the Government of India and the RBI in equal proportion. The bank has been statutorily empowered to draw resources from the Government of India, the World Bank, the multilateral and bilateral agencies, the open market and the National Rural Credit Long Term Operations Fund. Recourse can be taken to the National Rural Credit Stabilization Fund for converting short-term loans into medium-term loans when natural calamities occur. The RBI will provide resources for short-term operations to NABARD directly.

Management

NABARD's Board of Directors consists of a Chairman, Managing Director and 13 directors, who are appointed by the Government of India in consultation with the RBI. Among the 13 directors to be appointed, 2 are expected to be experts in rural economics, rural development, handicrafts, etc. 3 directors should be persons with experience in the working of cooperatives and commercial banks, 3 directors should be from among the directors of the RBI, 3 directors should be from the Government of India and 2 from the state government officials. The first Board of Directors was constituted by the Government of India under a notification issued by the Finance Ministry, dated March 19, 1983. Its first Chairman was Shri M. Ramakrishnayya, former Deputy Governor of RBI. Its second Chairman is Shri R.K. Kaul and Shri Sant Das is the Managing Director.

Functions

The functions of NABARD, as envisaged by the CRAFICARD, are as follows:

1. Development policy, planning and operational matters relating to credit for agriculture, allied activities, rural artisans and industries and other rural development activities.
2. Training, research and consultancy relating to credit for agriculture and rural development.
3. Refinance to commercial banks against term lending (medium- and long-term) and short-term accommodation for special purposes.
4. Refinance (short-, medium- and long-term) to the cooperatives and RRBs, including distribution and marketing cooperatives.
5. Direct lending singly or through consortium arrangements in special cases.
6. Coordination and monitoring of all agricultural and rural lending activities with a view to tying them up with extension and planned development activities in the rural sector.
7. Inspection of cooperatives and RRBs.
8. Advice and guidance to state governments, federations of cooperatives, the NCDC, etc, in regard to the cooperative movement and in close collaboration with the RBI and Government of India.

In short, NABARD will be the refinancing body for the entire rural lending system. If it were to find that the intermediary institutional credit arrangements for a specified purpose were not coming forth as expected, it would undertake direct lending to the public development corporations for productive and commercially viable activities. This is primarily a banker's bank, save in such exceptional circumstances.

Details

Commercial Banks

The interest on refinance of agricultural loans is 6.5 percent for minor irrigation and land development and 7.5 percent for other diversified purposes (6.5 percent for small farmers). Refinance can also be provided in respect of short- term loans given, on a selective basis, for integrated development projects.

Regional Rural Banks (RRBs)

Long-term refinance is provided to RRBs on terms and conditions similar to those applicable for commercial banks, as well as refinance (repayable over a period ranging from not less than 18 months to not more than 7 years) for medium-term loans given for agriculture and rural development. Short-term refinance is also provided at 3 percent below the bank rate. During July 1982–June 1983, RRBs having a loan business of Rs 8 crores and above as on March 30, 1982 could get refinance up to 40 percent of their outstanding eligible loans (that is, the total advances, less advances for which long-term refinance is availed of, consumption loans and advances against term deposit receipts). Their own involvement in the outstanding loans was, however, to be not less than 30 percent. RRBs having loan business of less than Rs 8 crores could get refinance up to 50 percent and their own involvement was expected to be not less than 20 percent in case of banks in existence for 5 years and above and not less than 15 percent in case of banks in existence for less than 5 years.

The level of involvement of an RRB and the refinance limit will be determined on the basis of its deposit resources, the balance retained with the sponsor bank and the realistic lending programmes. As and when the RRB affects sizeable recoveries from its primary borrowers, it is expected to repay the dues to NABARD. Advances against gold jewellery and silverware should not exceed 40 percent of the total outstanding loans, and advances to such category above this limit will not be eligible for refinance. Short-term loans granted to RRBs can be converted into medium-term loans for periods below 7 years under conditions of drought, famine, other natural calamities, military operations and enemy actions.

Land Development Banks/ Agricultural Development Banks

Refinance is provided for all approved schemes in agriculture and allied activities through debenture flotation duly guaranteed by the concerned state governments. The debentures will carry the same rates of interest as the refinance to commercial banks, category-wise.

Cooperative Banks

Refinance repayable within 18 months is provided to the State Cooperative Banks in respect of short-term working capital given for (a) agricultural operations, storage and marketing of agricultural produce; (b) any other activity for promotion of agriculture and rural development and; (c) production and marketing activities of artisans, small scale industries, village and cottage industries or persons or organizations engaged in handicrafts and other rural crafts. The interest charged on refinance is 3 percent less than the rate for agricultural operations and the bank rate.

The limits of refinance are fixed for agricultural purposes in relation to the financial position of central cooperative banks, their operational efficiency, and classification in audit, position of owned funds and ability to match the proposed borrowings by non-overdue loans outstanding against societies and lending programme.

Medium-term loans for periods not less than 18 months and not exceeding 7 years can be had for financing approved agricultural purposes and diversified activities at a rate of interest of 3 percent below the bank rate.

Long-term loans given by the scheduled commercial banks to agriculture and allied activities, small industries, village and cottage industries, processing industries, and marketing organizations are all eligible for refinance.

Uniform Discipline

One lending discipline uniformly applicable to all the participating institutions is recovery discipline. If 100 percent of eligible refinance were to be drawn, the participating institutions must have secured a minimum recovery of 65 percent during the preceding year (July–June), both in respect of short- and medium-term loans.

State Governments

NABARD

1. Provides comprehensive training to its own staff as well as to staff of participating banks for provision of and upgradation of skills and knowledge.
2. Takes over from the RBI the responsibility to coordinate with Government of India, Planning Commission, state governments and other all-India and state-level institutions engaged in development of small industries in the tiny and decentralized sector.
3. Monitors and evaluates the projects to ensure proper implementation.
4. Maintains a research and development fund which will be strengthened through contributions from its profits every year to promote research and explore innovative in lending consistent with the socio-economic policies of the government.
5. Acts as the agent of Government of India and RBI in business transactions in relevant areas.

It will be of interest to know that the NABARD Act did not define refinance, and therefore, it can leverage this factor to the advantage in the current scenario of banks innovating new products to finance agriculture and allied activities.

Note

1. B. Yerram Raju, 1969, AIRCS Report.

CHAPTER 9

Planning for Farm Credit: The NABARD Way

The public sector banks put out annual action plans under the aegis of NABARD and the Distinct Consultative Committees of Banks headed by the district collectors/district magistrates as chairpersons. At the micro-level, planning and monitoring mechanism for direct farm credit has just collapsed for the following reasons:

Crop loans can be granted to farmers under tie-up arrangements with the sugar mill, tobacco manufacturing companies, cold storages, seed companies or accredited input traders. Under the tie-up arrangements, the link agency—whether a trader or a sugar factory—would identify the beneficiaries to whom crop loans are to be extended for raising the specific crop, which would be collected by the relative companies after harvest, under an agreement to recover the loan amount to be paid to the bank by the farmer, from out of the amount payable to him for the produce so collected. A close liaison between the bank and the company with which a tie-up arrangement is to be entered into, is necessary. Some relaxations from the usual lending procedures are as follows:

1. No bank has been resurveying the villages allotted under SAP—a scheme introduced in 1989 following the recommendations of Ojha Committee Report—to assess the sectoral credit requirements at village level on an on-going basis.
2. The PLP prepared for each district by NABARD are, plans prepared for NABARD, of NABARD and by NABARD. The SAP of the scheduled commercial banks, their DCPs and the PLPs do not have much commonality.

3. This disharmony among the apex lending institution and grassroots-level financing institutions is widened by the government announcements of debt waivers and debt relief measures.
4. It would be worthwhile to analyse the harm done by the last measure to the farming community in the garb of helping them. This was done at a time when rural credit institutions were consolidating themselves in a positive direction, through proper planning. The gradual decline in private moneylending—most of it done by a few of the ruling elite, the rich farmer and trading community—could not be reversed without demoralizing the institutional framework. With one stroke of its pen, the Government of India did it in 1990—the massive loan write-offs. Apart from the debate as to who benefited from such write-offs, the measure has changed the psyche of the borrowers towards repayment of the bank. It is becoming extremely difficult to reverse this psyche.

   "The Committee is convinced that for the crop loans there is a substantial unfulfilled demand, which is being met by the moneylender, leading to the lower use of inputs and causing a loss of income to the farmers in both the situations."[1]

The banks, irrespective of the category to which they belong, were only waiting to find an honourable escape from their responsibility to the farm sector. The government provided a comfortable exit route. This was fuelled by the first report on Financial Sector Reforms that all was not well with the Directed Credit and therefore, there should be a drop in the Directed Credit Portfolio. While the author of the report did not recommend any drop in the mandatory aspect of credit flow for the agricultural sector, the messages were miscarried and there was over-enthusiasm on the part of commercial banks. Although the Parliament did not approve the recommendations relating to reduction in directed credit targets, the banks, in the garb of cleaning up their balance sheets, indulged in write-offs of the loss assets in the farm sector in a big way, between 1991 and 1994. There was a clear message not to maintain the tempo of farm credit disbursals. This saw a decline in net real farm credit.

Total disbursements of of All Scheduled Commercial Banks (ASBC) Credit for agriculture and allied activities were Rs 5,400 crores in 1993–94, and they showed an increase to Rs 1,60,690 crores in 2008–09. If you deflate it by the annual inflation rate and read the figures with the decline in the number of accounts annually by an average of 25,000 accounts, the position becomes very clear. The direct farm credit which should constitute 45 percent of the total priority sector credit (40 percent), or 18 percent of the total advances, slipped to 11.92 percent of the total credit in 2005–06. It has remained roughly at this level since 1994–95. The priority sector credit itself declined to 24.09 percent of total bank credit in 2011. Neither the RBI nor the Government of India pulled up the banks for the decline.

Short-term credit in the farm sector comprises of two components: (a) Usual crop loans, and; (b) Short-term loans supporting term lending portfolio. Investments in land development, minor irrigation, composite development projects, watershed development and waste land development projects would be requiring corresponding short-term working capital. The crop loan portfolio generally increases at the rate of 15 to 20 percent to the same set of farmers and crops, due to increase in input costs. Any increase over and above this percentage growth, supported by the increase in the number of accounts, should be reckoned as an increase in productive working capital portfolio in the farm sector. Look at the figures below.

Table 9.1 Variations in Number of Accounts and Net Bank Credit to the Farm Sector

Year	1997–98	1998–99	1999–2000	2000–01	2011–12*
Number of accts (in lakhs)	192	179	163	161	466
Percentage change amount (in Rs crores)	14.6	-9.8	-20.2	-1.2	2.89
Amount (in Rs crores)	34,305	40,078	46,190	53,685	4,66,391
Percentage variation	16.8	16.8	15.2	16.2	2.86
Percentage to net bank credit	15.7	16.3	15.8	15.7	10.6

Source: RBI statistics, www.rbi.org.

*Notes: *As on June 1, 2012; at annualized percentage variation.*

The steep decline in the number of accounts is compensated lately by the issuance of the KCC and an incremental volume for the same measure.

The incremental short-term credit flows hardly took care of the rise in input prices. The term loan disbursements, consequently, were not supported by the working capital. It is of common knowledge for any rational financing banker that this mismatch will lead to the creation of an unproductive asset. Instead of blaming themselves for the consequential NPAs, the bankers blame their clients! We also noticed in the previous paragraph that the number of accounts has declined compared to the number of farming clientele requiring institutional credit. This would mean that the banks did not entertain any new clientele in the farm sector. On the other hand, they drove away their existing clientele to the extent of 2.5 million accounts during 1991–2001. This could also mean that the banks could have written off as many farm accounts during this period.

Alarmed by this gradual fall, the government thought of providing another escape route for the banks in the achievement of the priority sector targets. This is through the Rural Infrastructure Development Fund (RIDF). In the first three branches, the Government of India passed on Rs 7,500 crores to NABARD to lend to the state governments to take up the unfinished/abandoned RIDF projects; the actual disbursements did not cross Rs 2,500 crores and all the state governments could not take advantage of this intervention. Out of Rs 18,545 crores sanctioned under the six tranches of RIDF till March 2001, Rs 9,251 crores was disbursed. This would only indicate that the farm sector was deprived of a credit flow to the extent of this shortfall.

Instead of insisting that the banks improve their direct lending portfolio to the farm sector, the Government of India diverted the allocable portfolio of priority sector lending. This suited the laggards in priority sector lending the most.

Having killed the goose that had started laying eggs, the RBI, in the wake of suicides of farmers in Andhra Pradesh, Karnataka and Maharashtra appointed a committee to look into the rural credit structure headed by the same person who was in-charge of it for years in the central banking institution. Without attacking the basic malaise that was afflicting the rural credit system, further tinkering was done.

Agricultural credit today suffers from high transaction costs and poor recoveries. The fact that our granaries are full reflects the neutrality of institutional credit flows to enhanced food production systems.

In the post-reform era, the RBI has imposed a cap on interest rates only on loans below Rs 25,000 and not beyond. Therefore, banks can no longer say that they are losing out a farm credit, if they follow principles of sound lending. Softer lending terms, in fact, need not lead to sacrifice of sound lending principles. Moral hazard occurs more because of the uninformed lender passing on credit to the informed borrower. In farm credit, this is all the more so.

In order to reduce the impact of moral hazard, dedicated centres were set up in the initial euphoria of the commercial banks' entry into farm credit during the 1970s. The State Bank of India had opened Agricultural Development Branches, set up the Agricultural Banking Divisions in intensive centre urban branches. Syndicate Bank pioneered in farm clinics, and Bank of Baroda had set up Gram Vikas Kendras, to site a few. During the first few years, these centres equipped with technical manpower of the then ARDC (now NABARD) had passed on credit to farmers with extension services. The recoveries were between 85 and 100 percent in the first few years, until the Integrated Rural Development Program (IRDP) came on the scene and a few states affected by natural calamities like floods, cyclones, and drought. It is not directed credit but forced credit, and the fanfare of the "loan melas" that diluted farm credit efforts. The link between credit and production snapped. Following the fall in recovery rate and the increase in transaction costs, banks thought that their dedicated centres for farm credits were luxury outfits. The technical personnel were allowed freedom to join the stream of general bankers because banks did not have a personnel policy that would weigh technical knowledge over a diploma from the Indian Institute of Bankers. Disheartened technical personnel gave up their extension efforts and jumped ship.

Today, the farm credit is disbursed and supervised by a rule book and not by an informed banker. The recipient is blamed. It is a real tragedy; banks did not develop a disaster management plan.

In the wake of a series of cyclones that struck the east coast in 1980, 1982, 1983, 1984, it became clear that the banks should not merely reschedule and postpone instalments but reissue the credit for replacement of lost assets at softer terms of lending. In order to facilitate these measures, commercial banks should charge commercial rates of lending for agriculture—carve out at 2 to 3 percent of the interest income into a long-term stabilization fund to meet calamity-stricken areas. Even after the revamp of the crop insurance scheme, this suggestion still holds valid.

The farmers are pretty sure that they cannot continue farming without timely and adequate availability of credit. It is strange that the number of accounts declined, there was only a marginal increase in direct farm credit, short-term credit did not increase in line with medium-term credit, but the food grain production increased from 198 million tonnes in 1996–97 to 241.56 million tonnes in 2010–11. This is a clear indication that the informal credit markets in the farm sector have started operating virulently.

If commercial and cooperative banks create an environment where farmers can develop confidence in them and purvey credit with extension services, farm credit will turn out to be a sound proposition with a reasonably high recovery rate.

Creating new institutions will not be an answer to the problems faced by the farmers—the Local Area Banks, for instance. Having created a massive rural branch network of commercial banks, the moribund cooperative banks, and the regional rural banks, it is but necessary to devote our attention to revamp them and not turn them into employee–centred institutions and deposit centres, meant for payment of wages and salaries.

"We treat the priority sector as a sacred cow and we starve it. It is not enough to make lending to agriculture mandatory; it must be profitable. Contrary to popular belief, farmers are more concerned with the easy and timely availability of inputs and services than their castes per se. Credit is one such service which must be made available in time and at the lowest possible cost. Perversely, we have allowed interest rates to be raised to make rural financial institutions viable. The result is that while some institutions are profitable, most borrowers are broke. Refinance at lower rates will help, but such lending will be truly profitable only when the transaction costs of banks are sharply reduced."[2] These transaction costs get reduced only when a group approach to supervised farm lendings takes place in an environment of mutual confidence.

There is a need for integration between land markets, credit markets and product markets and that would be possible only with proper policy formulation and integrating the complicated legal system impacting on the farm sector with the market mechanisms.

Sivaraman Committee, Ojha Committee and Khusro Committee had done an in-depth study into the problems afflicting rural credit. The RBI, Government of India and NABARD should constitute a working group to operationalize some of the suggestions incorporated therein and put them in the contemporary frame of reforms.

Suggested Measures

RBI should monitor the targeted flow of credit for the farm sector in terms of the credit plans prepared by the banks in accordance with the guidelines issued under the Service Area approach. Banks should resurvey the villages under their area of operation and prepare those plans which should specify the component they would be prepared to lend for the small and marginal farmers and the leaseholders/tenants/sharecroppers/oral tenants. At the time of the approval of the plan, the aggregate must be slightly in excess of the targeted flow for the sector, out of the anticipated total advances of each bank.

1. Each state government must ensure that the farmers are provided with the record of title to obviate any adverse selection.
2. Crop loans should have direct relation to the actual costs of cultivation prevailing in each district. Wherever possible, input supplies should be linked to credit through the KCC mechanism.
3. In respect of leaseholders/sharecroppers/oral tenants, crop loaning can be done under the group guarantee approach with a voluntary and self-reliant group of three to five members so that moral suasion would assure the repayments.
4. No bank shall grant term loans without the required sanction and assured timely release of the working capital/crop loan.
5. As far as possible, each farmer who gets a crop loan should be provided a term loan for silos or storage facility with easy and convenient instalment for repaying it. He should also be provided with a demand loan for storing the produce on a trust letter basis, for a period not exceeding four months after harvesting. The crop loan would get repaid out of the produce loan in this fashion. During the four-month period, the farmer would sell his produce in a period when the best price prevails or when the procurement takes place, whichever is earlier. Margins to be retained on the produce loans are to be market-driven. The interest rate for the crop and produce loan should, however, be identical and shall be market-related at the time of grant of the crop loan. The farmer should get the crop loan for the subsequent crop in the usual manner. If the trading intermediary is involved in the lending process with assured loan repayment backed by adequate collateral, such loans to the farmers should carry lower rates of interest than the direct crop loans, for the simple reason that interest rate is a function of risk.
6. The priority sector target should be disengaged from the contribution to RIDF and SIDBI bonds.

7. Farmers should also be sanctioned loans for either personal transport or produce transport depending upon the credit risk assessment by the concerned field staff, and any loan rejection, as in some banks, should be done only by the next higher authority, and the reason for rejection should be specified.
8. Classification of agricultural asset as NPA, particularly crop and demand loans, should be linked to failure to repay for two consecutive crop seasons. The normal rules for classifying a loan asset as NPA under agricultural segment will prove disastrous both for the borrowers and lenders. Unlike in other economic activities, agriculture is largely dependent on the vagaries of weather and wild fluctuations in markets. The farmer's decision to produce a particular crop is still not based on purely commercial considerations. The price of the output is also indeterminate. For all these reasons, the rules for classification of agricultural asset as NPA, need to be revised.
9. Since one part of the country or other is affected by natural calamities like floods, cyclones, droughts, earthquakes, etc, it is necessary that the banks should, in participation with the government—both centre and the states—set up a Disaster Relief Fund to provide relief to affected farmers in such calamities. As in USA, such a calamity relief fund at soft rate of interest of 3 percent, repayable in easy instalments, would greatly help farmers in conjunction with existing relief measures.

Notes

1. Gupta Committee, RBI, 1997.
2. Chidambaram, 1998.

CHAPTER 10

NABARD Needs to Rethink and Reposition: A Critique

The hopefuls on growth took a disappointing turn as we stepped into the Twelfth Five Year Plan and the uneven and tardy monsoon is likely to pull down agriculture growth for the year 2011–12 no more than 2.5–2.7 percent. The growth projections also went awry due to sustained fall in mining and manufacturing, and global sovereign debt-driven growth concerns. This is the time to look at institutional interventions we made during the last few decades, principal among them being NABARD, that became a nationalized bank in 2010.

In this regard, the expectations raised by the Expert Group (EG) on Agricultural Indebtedness (2007) deserve consideration: "NABARD, being an apex institution responsible for rural credit delivery, the EG recommends that efforts should be made to enhance further its developmental role helping the farmers to improve their credit-absorption capacity. NABARD should provide effective guidance and training to the banks in the formulation of projects related to agriculture and the rural non-farm sector." EG recommended that the unutilized banks' obligation towards priority sector lending to agriculture should be fully transferred to NABARD for direct lending or to issue of Rural Development Bonds by the central government instead of putting in RIDF. NABARD's supervision extends to both the RRBs and Rural Cooperative.

Credit Institutions

At this crucial juncture of India's consistently rising growth performance reaching a level of sustainability, a lot depends on how the debt-driven farm sector performs and what direction NABARD would be providing. It has, no doubt, built an enviable balance-sheet vis-à-vis other developmental banks on crucial indicators. As on March 31, 2010, NABARD's net worth (capital plus reserves) was Rs 12,674 crore and the Capital-to-Risk (Weighted) Assets Ratio (CRAR) was 24.96 percent, though almost a percent less than a year ago. There are 11.55 crore farmer households in the country, of which, 9.27 crore belong to small and marginal farmers. Institutional rural credit is accessible to only less than 50 percent of these farmers. It played a formidable role in SHG-Bank linkage programme, a forerunner for many of the micro- finance organizations and MFIs, and continues to innovate into reaching the grassroots of credit linkages. It has opened a new window to lend for debt-starved tenant farmers through the Joint Liability Groups, although this initiative is yet to find acceptance from its primary lending institutions (PLI). Metro and urban branches seem to have harvested more agriculture than the rural and semi-urban branches if we were to go by the Basic Statistical Returns (BSR) annual data of the RBI. Therefore, the time has come to leverage NABARD's formidable financial strength to revitalize the rural credit structure.

RBI, as regulator, and Government of India, as policymaker and owner of NABARD, should also look at this organization for a set of deliverables that would ensure financial stability, as the clients of NABARD occupy a near 15 percent space in the Indian financial system. "A stitch in time saves nine."

Apart from its developmental role, NABARD also performs certain supervisory functions in respect of cooperative banks and RRBs under the Banking Regulation Act, 1949. It may be noted that cooperative banks and RRBs have been in existence much before NABARD. Therefore, NABARD had to contend with some legacy issues for any clean-up it intended to do for these entities.

A few critical aspects that this article looks at with reference to the 2009–10 Annual Report, are the thrust of the balance sheet, the loan recovery performance of the primary lending institutions, financial inclusion effort, and the supervisory role of NABARD, and some suggestions.

Table 10.1 Credit Flow for Agriculture

Year	Coops Rs (Cr)	Total Rs (Cr)	Percentage
1982–83	2,275	3,685	61.7
1989–90	4,948	9,529	51.9
1999–2000	10,969	26,387	41.6
2009–10	57,500	3,66,919	15.7
Agency/Yr % distribution of ST Credit	2005–10	2008–09	2009–10
Coop	8.7	-4.7	25
Overall	18.5	18.6	21.5

When NABARD was created in 1982–83, cooperatives had a 61.7 percent share in the direct institutional credit to farm sector. By 2009–10, it gradually declined to just 15 percent. Sixty percent of the cooperative members are without credit. NABARD's investment portfolio is almost equal to its borrowings. Commercial banks take refinance more for gaining from treasury operations than for refinancing their agricultural credit portfolio.

Financial Scorecard

Through its main refinance portfolio to rural financial institutions (RFIs) and mobilization and disbursements under the RIDF, NABARD has over the past two decades built up a strong financial base. Its working capital and income showed marked improvement after taking over RIDF in 1995–96.

Half the 2010 balance sheet comes from RIDF, although it is only since 1995 that it entered NABARD portals. Deposits of RIDF resting with commercial banks constitute 85 percent of the total deposits and its lending constitutes 50 percent of the total. Four states take a little over 35 percent of it, reflecting a concentration risk. RIDF lending requires good PR rather than effective supervision at the ground level. RIDF takes away 44.2 percent of the lending and investment portfolio in 2010 compared to 38.6 percent in 2009, while its short-term credit refinance of Rs 24,073 crore is just 17.7 percent in 2010 compared to 14.2 percent in 2009 and investment credit refinance of 26.2 percent in 2010 is lower than what it was a year earlier at 28.2 percent. Twenty largest depositors have 82.38 percent of deposits and

20 largest borrowers have 51.94 percent of the credit exposure of NABARD. Top four NPA accounts total Rs 32.02 crore and its doubtful assets are Rs 44.02 crore again an increase from Rs 23.45 crore from the previous year (187 percent increase). Its direct lending portfolio attracted an increase in NPAs from Rs 8.88 crore in the previous year to Rs 17.6 crore (a hopping increase of 100 percent). This makes its net NPA claims in the total balance sheet, at less than 4 percent, totally irrelevant, and its leadership in rural credit less credible. Surprisingly, when its clients—Cooperatives and RRBs—carry a high concentration risk with increased provisions, NABARD carries only standard assets against them.

Provision coverage ratio is an important regulatory indicator. With respect to RRBs, as of March 31, 2009 the data reveals:

PCR range	<50%	50–70%	>70%
No. of RRBs	39	29	18

The more the provision, the less the efficiency in credit portfolio and the total number of RRBs. Thanks to further consolidation in 2009–10, it came down to 82 from the above 86.

Even the frequency distribution of states/ UTs according to loan recovery of State Cooperative Banks and District Central Coop Banks and RRBs as on June 30, 2009, reflect the declining credit discipline that became impervious, to the incentive of 1 percent for prompt recovery announced in the Union Budget that tried to reinforce credit discipline as a forerunner to equity principle in farm lending.

Percentage range	<40	>40 & <60	>60 & <80	>80
SCBs & DCCBs No. of banks	102	85	115	101
RRBs	0	5	40	38

Financial Inclusion

NABARD holds the two Financial Inclusion Funds recommended by the Rangarajan Committee, namely, the Financial Inclusion Fund and Financial Inclusion Technology Fund, each with Rs 500 crore corpus shared by Government of India, RBI, NABARD, in the ratio of 40:40:20. NABARD failed to gear up its efforts to make grassroots PACSs healthy and vibrant economic entities on the one hand, and effective instruments of financial inclusion on the other, because of conflict of interest between the two business lines, refinance and RIDF. Failure to take forward the Vaidyanthan Committee package to revive the cooperative sector is a solid case in instance. Its Annual Report cites just two examples down south—Thrissur and Kozhikode—the two may have got these laurels in spite of NABARD!

Supervisory Role

NABARD's tacit admission of the inefficiencies in the functioning of the cooperative credit structure year after year does not speak well either of itself or of the cooperatives. In fact, this is a cause of concern for the regulator, RBI, as the system NABARD supervises carries no less than 15 percent of space in the Indian financial system. From the point of view of financial stability and the systemic risk, more aggressive efforts and specific strategic initiatives are required on the part of NABARD.

Suggestions and Recommendations

Over the past two decades, NABARD has evolved into a strong and rural-sensitive apex developmental institution with a complete grassroots level understanding of the complexities of the agricultural and rural sectors. It is also a major shareholder in the Agricultural Insurance Corporation of India. It also has equity stake in National Commodity and Derivatives Exchange (NCDEX) in association with other national-level institutions such as ICICI Bank, Life Insurance Corporation of India (LIC) and the National Stock Exchange (NSE).

NABARD has a strong human resource (HR) and knowledge base but is underutilized to a large degree for want of strategic initiatives. Its consulting arm may be its revenue earning arm but it is better it gets rid of this role and concentrates on capacity building of its weaklings–PACSs. It should get into a mission mode to projectize the development of the rural cooperative financial system. NABARD should seek a further package for the cooperative sector but subject the sector to more rigorous monitoring mechanisms than the present one, and more rigid conditions for the revival package, for it is the cooperative credit system that has the capability to achieve the financial inclusion goals of the government and the RBI. It should also spearhead the legal reforms and governance reforms in the cooperative financial sector for rectifying the managerial and governance deficit.

NABARD should also divest its role from RIDF by carving out a subsidiary for the purpose if it is compelling enough or can issue rural development bonds as suggested by the expert group on agricultural indebtedness and leave the priorities to the states. All said and done, RIDF is just a risk-free rent seeking business. SHG and microfinance portfolio is another area that can become a subsidiary. The time has come for NABARD to reposition itself from the client perspective and rethink its role, consistent with the objectives, mentioned in the NABARD Act.

Reference

B. Yerram Raju, 1978, Kamath Committee Report, RBI.

B. Yerram Raju, 2012, *Inclusion Journal*, January–March, 3(1), pp. 73–75.

B. Yerram Raju, CRAFICARD, RBI.

CHAPTER 11

Agricultural Credit: Policy Issues and Problem Areas

The future growth of agriculture will depend on more efficient input-use, spread of low-cost technologies, raising crop productivity, increasing the capacity of the farmers to take risks, response to price-signals and adapting to change. There is, therefore, a pressing need to reshape agricultural policies in keeping with the new demands of the fast-changing economic environment.

Credit for the farm sector is a priority policy area. As mentioned earlier, the growing number of suicides by farmers, in different parts of the country in recent years, is largely the result of borrowing from non-institutional sources at very high rates of interest. In this chapter, we look at some of the issues and problems in ensuring adequate flow of credit to agriculture.

There are four main channels of credit available to a farmer: owner equity (which includes sweat equity and land equity); government; corporate sector and; institutional sources. The weak asset-base of the average Indian farmer and the inadequate targeting of government credit policy have led to greater dependence on non-institutional sources of credit.

Institutional Credit

An ideal system of agricultural credit would balance policy objectives with farmers' needs and the lending institution's feasibility within an overall framework of scarce resources. The main issues in shaping credit policy are: coverage (which farmers in which regions); quantum and terms of lending; regulation and recovery of loans. Timeliness is crucial in the supply of agricultural credit as crop production is based on seasonality and this factor has a major bearing on effectiveness of credit disbursed.

The flow of credit to agriculture involves lending for production and investment purposes. Crop loans are short-term in nature and are given for cultivation of crops before every season, to be re-paid after sale of crop produce. Agricultural term loans are investment credit loans, provided for land development, farm mechanization, developing irrigation systems, and other assets like plough bullocks, animal husbandry, aquaculture, apiculture, agro-forestry, etc, to be repaid over a period of time.

Before we turn to the data on agricultural credit in India, let us take a brief look at a recent statement reflecting the Government of India's views on the objectives of credit policy. The National Agricultural Policy (2000), states, "Progressive institutionalization of rural and farm credit will be continued for providing timely and adequate credit to farmers. The rural credit institutions will be geared to promote savings, investments and risk-management. Particular attention will be paid to removal of distortions in the priority sector lending by commercial banks for the agricultural and rural sectors. Special measures will be taken for revamping of Cooperatives to remove the institutional and financial weaknesses and evolving simplified procedure for sanction and disbursement of agricultural credit. The endeavour will be to ensure distribution equity in the disbursement of credit."

Increasing the flow of credit to agriculture became a major policy objective after 1969 with the nationalization of public sector banks and the stipulation of 40 percent of credit for priority sectors with a sub-target of 45 percent of it (or 18 percent of the total) for agriculture. This ushered in the phase of "social banking" to speed up attainment of development goals through widening the spread of credit delivery channels. In the 1950s, institutional sources accounted for around 8 percent of agricultural credit. There was overwhelming dependence of farmers on non-institutional sources such as professional moneylenders, landlords, traders and relatives. After 1969, there was a marked attempt to extend the reach of credit to agriculture with the huge resources that became available for this purpose. In 1970, nearly 85 percent of bank deposits and credit of of Scheduled Commercial Banks (SCBs) were with the public sector, a figure that rose to 90 percent by 1980. Expanding the reach of the banks geographically was one of the thrusts of credit policy in the 1970s. In 1969, barely 22.8 percent of public sector banks were in rural areas; while this had doubled to 44 percent in 1996, by 2011, the percentage of bank branches in rural areas declined to 37.4 percent.

Institutional sources of credit in 1969 included the Cooperative agencies (Banks and Cooperative Societies) and the Commercial Banks. In 1975, with the recommendation of the Narasimham Working Group on setting up RRBs there were three institutional sources for channelizing credit for agriculture–the Multi-Agency Approach to agricultural credit. NABARD set up as per the recommendations of the Sivaraman Committee (1980–81) is the apex body for rural credit institutions in the country.

Financial sector reforms were also part of the privatization-liberalization-globalization thrust which was initiated in 1991. The financial sector reforms were first introduced in the commercial banking sector, and, later, extended to the cooperative credit structure.

Pattern of Institutional Credit

The outreach of all rural credit institutions functioning within the Multi-agency framework showed a predominant position for Cooperatives in terms of outlets and borrowable accounts. In terms of share of rural credit disbursed, Commercial banks had the highest share, in 2005–06, of almost 68 percent, followed by Cooperatives with 22 percent and RRBs with almost 10 percent. However, Cooperatives had the largest share of Production credit (53 percent), followed by Commercial Banks (39 percent) and RRBs (8 percent).

However, despite the increase in absolute terms, the share of institutional credit to agriculture as a percentage of bank credit remained low and did not increase significantly despite the changes in the banking sector's lending norms brought about in 1969. The share of credit to agriculture was 2 percent in 1951 (when Agriculture's share in GDP was 55.5 percent) and rose to around 17.4 percent in 1990 (when the sector's share in GDP had declined to around 31 percent). There was a drastic reduction in the share of agriculture in bank credit thereafter to 11.8 percent in 1995, and has remained roughly at this level since then (11.92 percent in 2005–06) which is far short of the sub-target of 18 percent for agricultural credit.

One of the measures introduced in the banking sector to increase the flow of rural credit is the preparation by each bank of a Special Agricultural Credit Plan (SACP) with quarterly targets to be monitored by the RBI. Disbursements are to be targeted to increase by 25 percent over the previous year.

However, in a span of ten years, starting from 2000–01 till 2010–11, the share of commercial banks has substantially increased from 53 percent in 2000–01 to 74.5 percent in 2010–1. Even as percentage of agricultural GDP, institutional credit to agriculture has increased from 2.56 percent in 1970–1971 to 7.11 percent in 1980–1981 to 11.47 percent in 2000–01, and 32.21 percent in 2010–11. Although studies do suggest asymmetries in distribution of credit across farm size and across regions. But small farmers continue to resort to informal lenders (despite KCC), as the current system of institutional credit to farmers suffers from non-farmer friendly practices, delays in credit delivery and collateral problems.[1]

Keeping in view the importance of flow of credit to agriculture, in particular to the smaller borrowers who may not have the necessary assets as collateral, the banks have been advised to waive margin and security requirements for agricultural loans up to Rs 1,00,000. The "No Due Certificate" for small loans to SF/MF, sharecroppers, etc., have been dispensed with and instead banks have been instructed to obtain self declaration from the borrowers.

Figure 11.1: Sources of Institutional Agricultural Credit Percentage

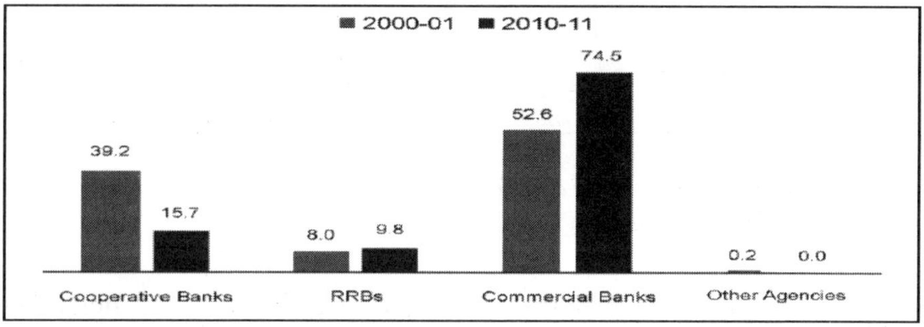

Source: Development of Agriculture and Cooperation.

The flow of agriculture credit since 2004–05 has consistently exceeded the target. Against a credit flow target of Rs 3,25,000 crore during 2009–10, the achievement was Rs 3,84,514 crore, forming 118 percent of the target. The target for 2010–11 was Rs 3,75,000 crore while the achievement on March, 2011 is Rs 4,46,779 crore. The agriculture credit flow target for 2011–12 has been set at Rs 4,75,000 crore and the achievement as on September 30, 2011, is Rs 2,23,380 crore.

Figure 11.2: Target and Achievement of Agricultural Credit from 2004–05 to 2011–12

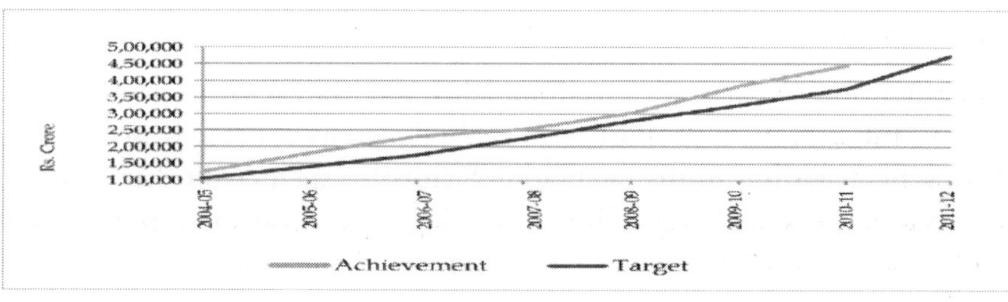

Figure 11.3: Flow of Institutional Credit to Agricultural Sector (Rs Crores)

Particulars/Agency	1998-99	1999-2000	2000-01	2001-02	2002-03	2003-04	2004-05	2005-06	2006-07	2007-08	2008-09	2009-10	2010-11	2011-12*
1	2	3	4	5	6	7	8	9	10	11	12	13	14	15
I. Production (ST) Credit														
Cooperative Banks	12514	14771	16528	18787	19668	22640	27157	34930	38622	40515	40230	56946	64527	47497
RRBs	1710	2423	3245	3777	4775	6088	10010	12712	16631	20715	22413	29802	37808	24976
Commercial Banks	9622	11697	13486	17904	21104	26192	36793	57640	83202	122289	147818	189908	216773	109049
Other Agencies	59	74	55	41	39	57	104	68	0	0	0	0	0	0
Sub Total (A)	23905	28965	33314	40509	45586	54977	74064	105350	138455	183519	210461	276656	319108	181522
II. MT/LT Total														
Cooperative Banks	3356	3489	4190	4737	3968	4235	4074	4474	3858	3169	5962	6551	5578	2335
RRBs	750	749	974	1077	1295	1493	2394	2511	3804	4099	4352	5415	6160	2484
Commercial Banks	8821	13036	14321	15683	18670	26249	44688	67837	83283	58798	81133	95892	115933	37039
Other Agencies	30	29	28	39	41	27	89	314	0	0	0	0	0	0
Sub Total (B)	12957	17303	19513	21536	23974	32004	51245	75136	90945	66066	91447	107858	127671	41858
ST+MT/LT Credit														
Cooperative Banks	15870	18260	20718	23524	23636	26875	31231	39403	42480	48258	46192	63497	70105	49832
RRBs	2460	3172	4219	4854	6070	7581	12404	15223	20435	25312	26765	35217	43968	27460
Commercial Banks	18443	24733	27807	33587	39774	52441	81481	125477	166485	181088	228951	285800	332706	146088
Other Agencies	87	103	83	80	80	84	193	382	0	0	0	0	0	0
Grand Total (A+B)	36860	46268	52827	62045	69560	86981	125309	180485	229400	254658	301908	384514	446779	223380

* Upto September, 2011

Source: Department of Agriculture and Cooperation, Credit Division and Union Ministry of Agriculture and Cooperation, New Delhi.

We need to look at where the credit flows actually reached through these country-wide credit institutions. Noticeably, the cost of production jumped up during the post-reform period due to increase in input prices with less and less money coming from institutional sources. Small producers resort to the 'distress surplus' and increasing costs of cultivation render them more dependent on large land owners for high interest loans. In a scenario of unequal distribution of land resources, small cultivators embracing of new technology deepens their dependence on those with economic, social and political power rather than leading to 'income diffusion'.[2] Thus, it is needless to do an elaborate exercise to rationalize the degree of support required from the institutional agencies.

Target Groups

Studies have found that credit flows found their way to areas where infrastructure existed. "Infrastructure for short-term credit flow rests not merely in existence of bank branches but in the facilitating factors for such credit dispensation: land records access and availability; technology, extension and input supplies in addition to irrigation.[3] In 1994, the 7 states with high-yielding major crops and the states of West Bengal and Gujarat received 94.3 percent of the total short-term credit flow of commercial banks in the country—a jump from 87.6 percent in March 1981.[4]

The per capita credit, or, to be more precise, per account credit, has not increased consistently with either the increase in the value of inputs or in the inflation. Between 1981 and 1991, the per capita farm credit increased from Rs 2,154 (1,513) to Rs 6,606 (5,063), to Rs 8,412 (6,606) in 1994, and to Rs 9,885 (6,785) in 2011 (figures in parentheses indicate the corresponding disbursements for small farmers).

Short-term credit for a small farmer is based on the scale of finance decided annually by the Technical Committee of the District Consultative Committee of Bankers in each district, providing data on local variations in the usage and value of inputs. The per capita crop loan for small farmers is lower than that of the other farmers, given the fact that banks are supposed to provide such loans on the basis of uniform scales of finance. Family labour, stored values of inputs like seeds and bio-fertilizers, are not accounted for properly in the case of small farmers.

The larger share of the southern states in the crop loans is on account of jewel loans getting included as crop loans, which account for as much as 60 percent. Jewel loans carry least risk in the agricultural credit portfolio of the banks. In the rest of the country, such jewel loans constitute no more than 10 percent of the crop loan portfolio. Still, the non-performing assets in agriculture, as indicated by the increase in the stock year after year, reflect poor credit management, although the NPA for agriculture is less than that for the other sectors.

Recovery of Loans

The author of financial sector reforms in this country, Shri Narasimham, stated, "The canons of sound banking and the objectives of social banking are not mutually contradictory."[5]

The issue of discipline in the borrowing clientele is inextricably linked to the following aspects:

a) Proper Appraisals: these have become mere arithmetical exercises of multiplying scale of finance for a crop indicated in the application with the acreage declared by the borrower
b) Proper Monitoring and Supervision: bankers do not find time to go to the farms or interact with the farmers during the currency of the loans, due to their preoccupation with a plethora of returns and records

c) Environment for farm production
d) Farmer behaviour or attitude conditioned by the political promises

Disaster Management[6]

Any institution desiring to lend to the farmers should be reconciled to the fact that the farmers are bound to face drought, cyclones, floods, holocausts, etc, sometimes one after the other, at other times, one or more of such disasters visiting together, depending on their location. While drought is a process, the others are events. It is easier to tackle process through appropriate advance planning, whereas in respect of events that occur suddenly, they have to be tackled after the event. It is, therefore, worthwhile for the credit analysts, agricultural policymakers and the implementing agencies to sit together and evolve a package to mitigate process-oriented situations like the drought watershed management, proper crop planning, etc.

Cyclones have a tendency to make soils saline and, therefore, in the post-cyclone situation, the lands have to be treated before they are brought back to normalcy; it may take even two or three seasons. The farmer faces a situation of loss of all assets, including homestead, sometimes loss of life/health. He has to incur huge investments for desalinization, raising fresh saline-resistant crops, purchase of cattle and other assets, apart from recouping his and his family's health. In the case of floods, though the farmer loses the investment, he has the scope to quickly regain it, as silt tops up the soil. Just broadcasting seed, other conditions favouring, may get him a bumper crop.

Unless the credit analyst has capabilities to respond to these situations with a sense of urgency and with a tolerable but accelerating financial package, the farmers' problems cannot be addressed appropriately and ably. The insurance agencies have to hedge most of these risks on location and situation-specific basis than on blanket coverage. A one-size shoe will not fit all. The fears and anxieties of both the lender and borrower are genuine and need to be addressed properly.

In USA, a Disaster Mitigation Fund is created with state participation for dispensation at 3 percent rate of interest to combat natural calamities. We may create such a fund with the state government, NABARD, lending agencies and insurance companies contributing to such a fund. The loans out of this fund are invariably utilized for converting the existing calamity-stricken assets into term loans repayable over a 10 year period. Depending on the frequency of visitation of the disasters, such loans may have to be given special dispensations, as the instalments of the regular loans and these converted loans overlap at the time of repayment. But extraordinary problems require extraordinary solutions.

Issues and Concerns

(a) Banks have disbursed nearly 94 percent of their agricultural credit in areas which have contributed nearly 65 percent of crop production. This did not in itself redound to their credit. They have neither taken a fair banking risk, nor demonstrated efficient risk management. They ended up with low profitability. The banks should modify their attitudes to farm lending and revamp their internal system.

(b) In the context of liberalization and financial sector reforms, deregulating the interest regime has opened up enough opportunity for cross subsidization within the farm sector itself. If all the credit requirements of the farmer—ranging from personal needs to the production, storage and marketing—are met on their own terms, the volumes offer scope for cost-effective supervision mechanisms and consequent profitability of lending operations.

(c) In a country of the size and diversity in the natural resource endowment, is credit subsidization, when restricted only to interest subsidy to small farmers in designated tracts but dovetailed with planned, regional development, injurious to economic growth? The producer subsidy is not as high as in the NIEs. The states of Orissa, eastern UP, Bihar, Assam and Madhya Pradesh have vast irrigation potential and virgin soils with potential for generating food surpluses that would eliminate starvation in both Asia and Africa in the next 2 decades, if only those states devote attention to creating dependable land records, promote technology, offer extension support, and allow cooperative agencies to perform in a truly cooperative way without any governmental interference. This thinking is reinforced by some of the utterances of leading agricultural scientists in the country.[7] A concern is being felt that the rapid growth from the Green Revolution is waning. Therefore, future agricultural growth needs to be broad-based with greater attention to the backward regions, especially in the central and eastern parts of India.[8] Coupled with systemic changes in the lending organizations, credit subsidy in some measure, may lead to faster agricultural growth in these hitherto undeveloped states.

(d) Regarding equity, the credit deployed by the commercial banks to account holders who were small farmers received 22.92 percent of the total direct credit flow in 2006–07, while marginal farmers received 24.69 percent. These figures invariably provide a convenient statistical base for the commercial banks to argue out their bias to the small farmer while extending credit to the farm sector. Every account, grouped under this head, however, need not belong to a small farmer. This distortion has occurred because of the interest subsidy and other concessions announced in favour of the small farmer clientele. Does the correction to this malady lie in altogether doing away with the subsidy? As suggested by the committee on financial system, redirecting the subsidies to proper target groups like the small farmers and specific regions with a reduction in the directed credit portfolio (from 40 to 25 percent of the total credit), may provide an answer. Modifying the direction and setting the target would call for a thorough inquest. Adhocism is no answer to the anxieties and concerns in this regard.

(e) The decentralized credit planning mechanism introduced through the service area plans as a refinement over the erstwhile district credit plans has not functioned well. The commercial bank branch staff, which was expected to visit the villages annually, as also update the database for assessing the potential, and for dovetailing the demand for credit for poverty-alleviation and employment-oriented programmes, failed to perform this task. The banks' supervisory mechanism failed to monitor these aspects as they did not recognize this exercise as a tool for improving the qualitative performance of rural credit portfolio.[9]

Measures Suggested to Improve the System of Agricultural Credit

C. Subramaniam, former Union Minister for Finance as also Agriculture, while delivering the J.V. Reddy Memorial Lecture in 1988, stated, "Looking ahead, two major problems for the credit structure can be defined. One has to do with discipline and the other with equity...Despite all exhortations, the commercial banks seem unable to reach out adequately to the weaker sections unless backed continually by concessions and guarantees from the government. Both these aspects of sustained self-reliance for credit institutions and ability to serve weaker sections will need special attention if the objectives set out are to be fulfilled."

Some of the measures which can strengthen the system of agricultural credit in terms of the policy objectives are:

1. Increasing credit allocations to agriculture. Since agriculture contributes a little over 14 percent of GDP, its share of credit within priority sector lending should be proportionate. It is not clear on what basis the sub-sector loan target of 18 percent has been arrived at.
2. The credit flow target for agriculture by institutional agencies should be in terms of number of farmers benefited rather than in terms of finance disbursed.
3. Area under cultivation in small and marginal holdings has increased to over one-third of total area. More than 50 percent of agricultural production comes from small holdings. Therefore, small and marginal farmers should get the benefit of economic reforms. If one looks at the data on recoveries, the repayment rate has been higher for small farmers than for other sectors.
4. The absence of land records affects the flow of credit. It is necessary to improve and update the database for land holdings.
5. The financing or credit flow to sharecroppers and leaseholders has not received attention from policymakers. About 60 percent of cultivators are not owners of land and their credit needs have to be met by the institutional agencies.
6. A coordinated approach by the various credit agencies needs to be formulated for efficient flow of credit to agriculture. At present, too many agencies are spread too thinly
7. A synergistic relationship needs to be developed between the institutional agencies and the farm sector. At present, banks' capacity and willingness to take risks do not match.
8. Agriculture-industry linkages should be promoted.
9. While the perspective plans provide an opportunity to take stock of the situation at the end of every year, none of the perspective plans had any demonstrable effect on the lending pattern of the credit retailing to the farm sector.
10. RBI should divest its routine role of rural credit planning to the specialized institution, namely NABARD, and should perform only a supervisory role.
11. NABARD's role as a refinance agency is being shortened. The institution has to re-define its role and has to consider the way the farm sector has to cope with the WTO challenges. Its predisposition with the

cooperative sector also requires a fresh look. NABARD should move into the position of a solution-provider.

12. HRD efforts in cooperative banking are not enough. NABARD has to refurbish its governing structure and fulfil the governance aims of its agriculture and development functions.
13. Investment in critical areas like biotechnology and information technology as a tool for activating markets, will require specific funding directly from NABARD.
14. There needs to be more professionalism in the apex functions to be performed by NABARD, by hiring consultants for additional inputs for better attainment of the policy objectives.
15. Each rural and semi-urban bank branch should plaster their walls with the terms and conditions under which the credit facilities for crop and investment purposes would be available and under what terms and conditions.
16. The new enactment of the Securitization and Reconstruction of Financial Assets and Enforcement of Securities Interest (SARFAESI) Act, 2002 has done great injustice in restricting the commercial banks to proceed against land as collateral security for realizing their dues. Non-realizable securities henceforth should be unacceptable to these banks. Agriculturists and agro-based industrialists can offer their land holding alone as the security. Despite all that is discussed above, the commercial banks may drag their feet still further for lending to agriculture and agro-based industries. But these are precisely the activities that deserve attention if we want to reach the goals of the Tenth Plan.
17. Interest rates fortunately are on the decline and the RBI's recent directive to charge differentially for this sector at sub-PLR, puts off any discussion relating to this issue for the time being.

Can we de-link credit for agriculture in its broadest sense, from land as primary or collateral security?

Can we regard the farmer as equivalent to any salaried employee in the organized sector and extend credit for all his requirements through multiple lines of credit?

Can the land rights (owned and lease-hold) be converted into a cognizable equity in his asset portfolio?

Kisan Credit Card Scheme

With the aim of increasing access to short-term credit by farmers, the KCC scheme was introduced in 1998–99. All institutional agencies have taken up the scheme throughout the country. In 2008–09, a total of 358.63 lakh KCC were issued which involved credit sanctions amounting to Rs 46,669 crores. In terms of break-up by institutional agencies, commercial banks accounted for 51.98 percent of KCCs, followed by RRBs (25.51 percent) and cooperative banks (22.49 percent). Personal insurance cover for accidental death or permanent disability for KCC holders has been finalized.

National Agricultural Insurance Scheme (NAIS)

Since agriculture is a highly risky activity under Indian conditions with a large degree of rainfall dependence and crop loss through pest attacks and natural calamities, a comprehensive system of insurance is of utmost importance. The Comprehensive Crop Insurance Scheme (CCIS), which was in operation since 1985, has been replaced by NAIS since the rabi season of 1999–2000. The Scheme is being implemented by the General Insurance Corporation on behalf of the Ministry of Agriculture, Government of India in 21 states and Union Territories.

NIAS is available to all farmers regardless of size of land holding or level of indebtedness. Its coverage extends to all food crops (cereals, millets and pulses), oil seeds, and horticultural crops. A 50 percent subsidy in the premium is given to small and marginal farmers.

The area covered by the scheme in 2008–09 was 2.65 million hectares with about 1.91 million farmers.

1. Crop insurance needs special attention. Increased coverage, reduced premium, lesser burden on farmers through sharing of premia, speedy settlement of claims, etc, are some of the issues that need to be addressed.
2. The GIC should put out the warranty conditions and the threshold norms in a transparent fashion so that the claims could be put up properly and well within time, apart from enlarging the coverage of insurance to new crops and new sectors. The premium rates for the crops and other allied activities have to be still brought down although the companies may turn down this idea on the plea that the risk weight age carries the price along with it. Under these circumstances, the

Government of India, state governments and the financing institutions have to bear the burden of high premia in some agreed proportion.

Conclusion

Future policy focus has to be on revamping the entire rural credit structure. Despite a long history of more than three decades of prioritizing institutional credit flow to agriculture, the results on the ground do not indicate the success of credit policy in achieving its objectives. The majority of farmers continue to experience lack of access to credit at a time when their problems are mounting due to the economic and environmental pressures they face while carrying out their farming activities.

In the present post-liberalization context, a farmer faces challenges on several fronts. He needs more credit for crop production and investment, more skills to use the emerging technologies, more options to cope with risk and change, and more information to be better equipped to face new development. He, therefore, has to have assured access at his farm-gate to quality inputs, seed, fertilizer, pesticides, power, water, extension services and the appropriate technology package to enable him to undertake agricultural production with reduced risk. Credit is the key input for the Indian farmer and will remain so for some time to come. Revamping the credit structure to meet farmers' needs should be the thrust of agricultural policy for the next decade.

With liberalization, the state's role does not diminish. Capital formation in agriculture will remain a major area for state intervention in the future. Without this, the future development of the agricultural sector will be seriously threatened. Agricultural research, which now claims a miniscule proportion of GDP—around 1 percent—needs to receive increased allocations. It is to be noted that, "The achievements of the Indian agricultural research system so far in respect of raising yields and reducing variability in the unfavourable agro-climatic regions are not comparable with those realized for the favourable environments in the early years of the Green Revolution. The tools of emerging biotechnology…offer significant possibilities for breaking these barriers."[10] Research in institutions such as ICAR and agricultural universities should be directed in tune with what the market wants. The emphasis, in the future, will be on low-cost technologies, post-harvest technologies, new strains, and new territories around the globe. The state's role will be crucial in these efforts to encourage investment flows into emerging areas. This will have a catalytic role on the private sector.

Agro-industry venture capital will become an area to explore. Commodity futures will also assume great importance under WTO. The training and education of players in the market, with full use of existing resources, and also drawing from capital markets and derivatives, will be needed. Economic liberalization can be expected to result in an increase in requests for aid for agricultural markets. Indian regulated market laws over-specifies conduct. It is a highly ideological law stipulating that one contractual form is efficient. "The law needs to be reformed so as to state what is unacceptable conduct, thereby freeing a larger legitimate contractual space."[11]

Enforcement has to be standardized and powerful, and at the same time should have positive incentives for compliance. This would facilitate farmers converting their farm-stead into viable enterprises eligible for financing on their own merit.

Financing marketing activity in the agricultural sector is as complex and varied as agricultural activity itself, with a large number of buyers and sellers associated with imperfections in market information and myriad regulatory instruments. All the regulatory laws should be consolidated into an Act. A compendium for compliance should be prepared in the mean time by NABARD to act as a guide. Propensity Appraisal System should be introduced to finance the farmer, when the calendar of assets in various forms resting with farmer, could be lent safely.

Notes

1. B. Yerram Raju, 2012, Indian Agriculture Report.
2. Kalpana, Wilson, 2002, "Small Cultivators in Bihar and 'New' Technology", *Economic and Political Weekly*, 37(13).
3. Raju, 1991.
4. Raju, 1997.
5. Narasimham, 1995.
6. Raju, 1985, "Disaster Management: Role of Financial Institutions", Economic Times, 25, January.
7. Gulati, 1989.
8. Singh, 1995.
9. Raju, 1993, "A strategy for sustainable projects for the poor", *NABARD Newsletter* Vol 4(5), August 1, Mumbai.
10. C.H. Hanumantha Rao, 1989.
11. Barbara Harriss-White, 1996, *A Political Economy of Agricultural Markets in South India*, pp. 307–337, 341.

CHAPTER 12

Priority Re-prioritized or De-prioritized?

Report of the Working Group on Priority Sector Credit—A Critique

The concept of "priority sector" in commercial banks' advances has been in existence ever since the first lap of nationalization of banks. However, the committee on Financial Sector Reforms, 1991 (Narasimham Committee-1) sought a review of directed lending portfolio clothed in priority sector as it perceived that extraordinary support should be extended to certain sectors only, "to correct the perceived imperfections in the credit market". It also believed that "such intervention should be seen as temporary rather than a permanent feature". However, the Government of India differed with this part of the recommendation and the RBI has been defining and redefining the components of the priority sector, adding or deleting some sub-sectors or modifying the sectors. Banks have been feeling uncomfortable lending under this portfolio anyway. Public sector banks, unable to express any dissent over such social overtones to the lending because of the government's control over them, have been calling for a review. This eventually found expression in the declaration of the Governor, RBI, in the Monetary Policy Statement of 2011–12, to constitute a Working Group (hereafter referred to as the Nair Committee) to re-examine the existing classification, and suggest revised guidelines with regard to priority sector lending and related issues. Ever since 2005, financial inclusion is the new bogey under which social banking has been gaining currency, and the priorities in banking have been juxtaposed with the Know Your Customer (KYC) norms compulsively, due to introduction of technology on the one hand and technology on the other. It is this context that prompted the Nair Committee to mention:

"Going forward, the country's vision is of universal financial access through affirmative financial inclusion, which will mainstream the marginalized by ensuring 'access'. Until we achieve the desired level of financial deepening at all levels of society, in rural as well as urban areas, the need for directed lending will continue as a necessary lynchpin of the macro policy framework."

Structural inefficiencies and geographical incongruities cannot find appropriate response in sectoral allocations of credit. This paper would like to examine the trends in rural and urban banking and see whether the redefined priorities fit into the emerging requirements of the less endowed population of the economy. We would like to see, in the light of the recommendations of the Nair Committee, whether the rechristened priorities would better serve the objectives before them by adopting population segment approach and institutional reform instead of sectoral approach.

The Committee deserves compliments for doing away with DRI credit and for suggesting credit guarantee for agriculture credit. The rest of the report of the committee deserves a thorough re-look as the entire report seems to help banks more than their lesser-endowed clients, who deserve a better deal than the one they currently have.

About 72.2 percent of about a 122 crore population lives in around 6,38,000 villages, and the remaining 27.8 percent in about 5,480 towns and urban agglomerations. About 74.4 percent of the population is literate, with 84.01 percent males and 65 percent females falling under such category. BSR data of RBI has interesting insights into the trends in which deposits and credit have been moving during 2006–10 (we have taken 2006 as the year for this exercise since the clarion call for financial inclusion was given in 2005) on demographic profile. The claims of commercial banks' achievements in the designated priority areas also throw up interesting conclusions.

Table 12.1 Metro/Urban/Semi-Urban/Rural Banking Profile (As on June 30, 2011)

Geographical Segment	No of bank branches	Deposits (Rs Cr.)	Credit (Rs Cr.)	CD ratio (%)
All India	90,147	53,70,669	40,38,310	75
Top 6 metros	9,214 (10%)	24,40,357 (45%)	22,34,486 (55%)	92
Metro Centres	15,857 (18%)	30,31,527 (56%)	26,78,238 (66%)	88

Top 100 Centres (inclusive of metro centres)	24,225 (27%)	37,21,662 (69%)	31,68,351 (78%)	85
Urban Centres (inclusive of metro & other centres)	33,774 (38%)	41,46,338 (77%)	33,58,102 (83%)	81
Semi-urban Centres	22,860 (25%)	7,27,226 (14%)	3,82,678 (9%)	53
Rural Centres	33,513 (37%)	4,97,105 (9%)	2,79,530 (7%)	56

Source: RBI Annual and BSR Reports.

Even against all the claims by commercial banks over financial inclusion, rural and semi-urban centres, where 72 percent of the 122 crore population resides, happen to have a share 23 percent of deposits and 16 percent of credit. It is in these areas that the scope for agriculture and non-farm credit exists. Let us see how the agriculture credit has been moving during the last four years. Farmers, according to the RBI data, seem to be harvesting more in metro and urban areas than in the rural and semi-urban areas.

Table 12.2 Population-Wise Outstanding Credit—All Scheduled Commercial Banks in Agriculture From 2006 & 2010 (Rs Cr.)

	Mode of Finance	2006		2010	
		No. of Accounts	Agrl. Credit Outstanding	No. of Accounts	Agrl. Credit Outstanding
Rural	Direct	1,69,65,209 (58%)	59,732 (35%)	2,36,39,133 (55%)	1,35,414 (35%)
	Indirect	4,03,005 (1%)	4,386 (3%)	9,80,153 (2 %)	14,720 (4%)

Semi-Urban	Direct	93,51,917 (32%)	39,891 (23%)	1,36,97,855 (32%)	94,681 (24%)
	Indirect	170,894 (0.5%)	3,776 (2%)	5,68,342 (1%)	14,029 (4%)
Urban	Direct	19,39,273 (7%)	15,640 (9%)	31,39,110 (7%)	42,748 (11%)
	Indirect	57,355 (0.19%)	8,174 (5%)	1,83,060 (0.42%)	24,819 (6%)
Metros	Direct	1,61,794 (0.5%)	9,298 (5%)	5,25,539 (1%)	24,004 (6%)
	Indirect	18,666 (0.06%)	31,783 (18%)	36,637 (0.08%)	39,879 (10%)
Total Agrl. Credit		2,90,68,113	1,72,683	4,27,69,829	3,90,297

Source: ibid.

While the shares in number of accounts in rural areas remained either constant or marginally varied during 2006–10. The percentage increase in number of accounts under direct agriculture credit portfolio in rural areas is around 39 percent, in urban areas it is over 60 percent, and in metros it is over 300 percent. In terms of outstanding credit, direct agricultural credit more than doubled during the same period in rural areas. It moved up by over 180 percent in urban and metro areas together. Indirect agricultural credit moved up in all the areas significantly as it affords adequate risk protection through confident collaterals, though there is no segmental information about the status of NPAs in this portfolio to comment on its performance. NPAs data is shown only against agricultural sector and not in direct and indirect portfolios separately. Even according to the data put out in the report, direct agriculture credit has been declining both at the hands of the public and private sector banks, particularly during the last four years, while the government has been claiming that credit to agriculture has doubled in its reports. Where the credit galloped—agriculture credit—is therefore in urban and metro areas. Arm-chair lending assumed priority over the directed lending portfolio for the simple reason that persons to man the systems on one side, and to go to the field to do due diligence in agriculture and MSEs on the other, have a great mismatch. The new recruits posed new challenges to the HR portfolio of the banks. Most of them are proving efficient and responsive to systems and not to the handling of lending portfolios of rural and semi-urban areas. The committee has overlooked this aspect in making its recommendations. It is people who deliver credit and accept deposits, and honing their attitudes and skills continue to pose a serious challenge to the banking industry.

State-wise data reveals, interestingly, that 10 states in the country—the 4 southern states, Maharashtra, Punjab, Haryana, Gujarat, West Bengal and Uttar Pradesh—take a share of almost 80 percent of agricultural credit, and 11 states, with Delhi added, take a similar percentage of Micro and Small Enterprises (MSE) credit. Any re-setting of priorities should have taken into consideration this scenario and corrections suggested. Unfortunately, the Nair Committee appears to have missed this aspect. By combining direct and indirect agriculture credit, banks get the facilitation to show better performance in the so-called priority sector. Disbursement of agriculture credit—direct to the farmers—takes place in areas where irrigation facilities are available in abundance. Drought-prone areas suck the credit where watershed management and drought-proofing measures have taken place. If the objective of re-prioritization were to ensure that the credit flow to the needy, in time, and also in tune with the growing requirements of input use, the committee would have done a deeper analysis before re-allocating the portfolio. The committee would do well to revise its recommendation that 9 percent of agriculture credit should go to small and marginal farmers. The committee defined agriculture finance saying, "Agriculture finance will encompass the entire gamut of agricultural and allied activities, pre-harvest, post-harvest activities and the entire value chain of farm produce, including transport, storage creation, grading, packaging, processing up to the market-end without any distinction between direct and indirect categories." The implication of this definition is that the high-value credit in post-harvest operations would take the meat of the allocated priority sector, again landing the farmers in credit stress. Farmers requiring credit for pre-harvest and for investment in land development and farm machinery are bound to suffer in the process of implementing this prioritization. This does not mean that we do not endorse the holistic approach to meeting the credit requirements of this sector. All we would like to say is that farmers seeking production credit would cry hoarse and the suicides would not end.

Providing a window of opportunity for default through investments in RIDF/SIDBI has done harm to the intent of prioritization. Levying penalties, that too through interest arbitrage, is a retrogatory step. RIDF has become the golden egg of NABARD. In fact, NABARD should hive off RIDF into a separate subsidiary and dedicate itself to lending and refinance for cooperative and commercial banks respectively. This single step has the prospect of undoing the damage to institutional finance for agriculture. The expert committee (Professor Radhakrishna, Chairman) recommended doing away with the linkage to RIDF. The banks shall achieve the Priority Sector (PS) credit targets particularly because the PSLC is introduced.

Those that fail to lend for agriculture and MSE credit sub-targets should carry an annual penalty, the size of which should be such as to discourage them from indulging in this luxury. The entire section relating to shortfall and the RIDF is, therefore, redundant and this window of opportunity for the commercial banks should be closed if the committee is serious about the allocations, prioritization and financial inclusion.

As share of infrastructure continues to grow and crowd out priority sector lending, linking agriculture and priority sector lending to ANBC, which includes infrastructure, would be counter-productive, as the credit absorption capacity of the 'low value-high volume' agriculture and MSME is considerably low vis-à-vis infrastructure.

The committee would have done better if it had dealt with the role of the cooperative sector in reaching the last mile in the agriculture and MSE portfolios than pitching their fork against the NBFCs. While both these sectors have their respective roles, the financial support in terms of equity would be available more for the latter than the former. There should have been a categorical recommendation related to the change of management of the cooperative sector and the imminent need of the state and central governments to bring about legal changes and recapitalization until they absorb the managerial, technological, accounting and systemic changes of Vaidyanathan Committee, to become part of the mainstream of the Indian financial system. In the Financial Stability Report of the RBI, cooperative banking has been recognised as an important part of the Indian financial system although its attention to making it part of mainstream banking, falls short of requirements. Mismanagement and mis-governance for over 60 years of its existence, cannot be expected to be rectified overnight without legal, structural and attitudinal changes.

Activities that are commercially acceptable lines of lending for commercial banks need not fall under the priority as commercial banks take to them like fish taking to water and they do not require either interest SOPS or subsidies and for fewer directions. It is in this context that the lending to *adithiyars* is placed out of the priority sector silo.

Small and marginal farmers hold 83 percent of the operational holdings but contribute to only 23–24 percent of production. When credit is related to inputs and investments in farming, how can 50 percent of the total allocation to these sections help rectify the imbalance unless such percentage is related to the number of accounts? In terms of credit flow, the 50 percent allocation to SF, MF would suffer non-achievement. As regards tenant farmers, the JLF has been almost a non-starter, despite NABARD's thrust and some states like Andhra Pradesh dabbling with a hackneyed legislation. Therefore, the committee should re-visit this part of the recommendation and also revise its perspective of priority from mere sectors to areas; the banks should be enjoined upon to lend 80 percent of the total number of accounts and 60 percent of the ANBC to the redefined sectors in rural and semi-urban areas, and 10 percent in urban and metro areas in terms of the number of accounts, and 40 percent in terms of the amount lent (this 40 percent would be mostly the presently categorized indirect lending for agriculture and the MSMEs). Corporate agriculture should be kept out of the purview of priority allocation.

The committee acknowledges that, "Out of the 74.97 million SFMF in the country, only about 46.3 percent, that is, 34.70 million farmer households have access to credit, either from formal or informal sources. The most important source of loan for all farmer households in terms of percentage of outstanding loan amount, is banks, which is 36 percent." As of March 2011, the total number of loan accounts of SFMF with domestic scheduled commercial banks was approximately 23 million. Considering that a farmer, on an average, may have more than one account with bank(s), it may be deduced that only around 15 percent to 20 percent of small and marginal farmer households are availing loans from public sector and private sector banks. In any case, 23 million SFMF accounts would not have covered 34.70 million farmer households of SFMF. This is so despite the commercial banks' claims to have doubled credit for agriculture during 2008-11.

While the data on farm households is right, the number relating to those having access to credit would appear patently a conjecture, as the banks put out information only on the number of accounts and not on number of farmers. The committee's assumption in this regard, needs revision. In case the committee still considers that their assessment is right, they should at least consider not granting any concession for not achieving this target through investments in NABARD RIDF. In fact, it would be better if the target is revised to number of SF, MF, JL accounts; it should be 50 percent of the total farmer accounts under production credit, monitorable at the state level by NABARD on a quarterly basis. This measure, coupled with a minimum of 9 percent of ANBC to such category, should also be reviewed at the end of 2 years by the RBI. We are of the opinion that 4 years is too long a period for banks to reach the meagre 9 percent target. Two years should be adequate.

Micro and Small Enterprises

While we are in agreement with the committee in regard to the allocations for the MSE credit, we are unable to see the merit in classifying education loans under this category. If loans to students belonging to the economically disabled communities shall be given as allocated credit, it should be separately mentioned.

Weaker Sections

While we agree with the contention that separate allocations for the weaker sections does not make sense either from the angle of distributive justice or economic exigency, the classification is fraught with high risk. Category (a) has already been allocated 9 percent of ANBC, meaning thereby that the rest of the categories (b) to (j) would be just 1 percent of ANBC, as the total allocation for the weaker sections is 10 percent of ANBC. The Parliamentary Committee that has already expressed its displeasure of the achievements of banks in this sector is likely to reassert itself in this regard. Further, the recommendation under this head reads as follows:

> "Loans granted under (a) to (i) mentioned above to persons from minority communities."
>
> It would make a more sensible reading if it is mentioned as "loans given to minority communities up to the specified loan limits for the categories (a) to (i)."

Recommendation 3.12: How can the committee mention cooperative banks as non-banking financial intermediaries? This needs revision.

While we agree with the committee on on-lending targets to the NBFCs, PACS, MFIs, keeping the underlying asset in view, it would be prudent to consider exclusions categorically, like loans extended against gold jewellery by NBFCs, and other intermediaries may continue to be excluded as a part of priority sector classification. Likewise, all gold loans of commercial banks shall be excluded from the purview of priority sector. PSLCs are a good intervention and the experimentation may prove successful in reaching the last mile in priority sector credit.

Eligibility Criteria

While the committee did well in stipulating the eligibility criteria, mandating the commercial banks to lend collateral free advance up to Rs 1 lakh only falls short of the CGTMSE guidelines. There must be consistency with the regulations, with respect to the MSE sector. With respect of other sectors, if the intention of the committee was to establish another guarantee organization to deal with the farm sector, as expressed earlier, then the collateral-free advance limit should be related to the economic level of the activity on the one hand and the ability of the borrower to extend collateral on the other. The SARFAESI Act does not recognize farm land as acceptable collateral and taking this into consideration, as also the tenancy laws, while lending for the tenant-farmers, the committee should reconsider this recommendation. Our suggestion is that all agricultural production loans up to Rs 1 lakh and investment loans of any category up to Rs 2 lakh (both these categories should be inflation-indexed annually for appropriate revisions) and MSEs up to Rs 10 lakh should be made collateral-free. Banks that take collateral security should be doing so only at the cost of not recognizing them when the loans fail for one reason or the other. The SARFAESI Act also should be amended to this effect. Otherwise, the effect of this recommendation of extending collateral-free advances to the hitherto neglected sections would not be in the interest of inclusive growth.

Micro Finance

1. While reiterating the recommendations and approach of the Malegam Committee regarding the treatment, pattern and distribution of MFI loans, the committee should reconsider its recommendation relating to the payment of insurance premium as we feel that such premium should be part of the overall 26 percent of jewellery cost of the loan to the primary borrower.
2. There should not be any penalty for delayed payment. Non-penalty could lead to licentiousness on the part of beneficiaries. It depends on how you define "delay". Delay should be within a maximum of two times the scheduled repayment period (weekly repayments—2 weeks; fortnightly—a month; monthly—2 months). This would ensure no licentiousness on the part of the beneficiaries.

Documentation

Recommendations in Para 4.3: Why should RBI get into this micro management? Documentation would depend on the securities available to the lending banker and the type of loan—short-term within the 3 year period, or above 3 year period. In case a loan is granted and documents are taken for loans below 3 year period, the renewal of documents has to be done well before the expiry period of previous documents. Suitable diarizing and pop-ups on the system should prompt field officers for these actions. It is desirable that RBI leave such issues under the required prudential management of the commercial banks.

Management Information System

It is highly laudatory that considerable attention has been rightly devoted to the MIS, for the simple reason that the MIS absorbs considerable cost of administering priority sector credit. But the point missed out is the origination issues in data. Data misreporting or convenience-reporting arises on account of facilitation that its origination provides. For example, KCC are issued but the related disbursal is done only through the Agriculture Cash Credit in the general ledger of the bank. Therefore, loans disbursed under KCC, or for that matter General Credit Card (GCC), are reflected both under the KCC and GCC data and semis, or under envisaged Priority Sector Management Information System (PSMIS). Therefore, all such credit card information data should be treated as stand-alone information and should not be aggregated under any PSMIS. Second, product-wise accounts are not generated either at the subsidiary or general ledger. Unless banks are enjoined upon to generate subsidiary ledgers in the system for the existing PS products and new products, as and when created, the MSE and agriculture loan data are prone to duplication in the PSMIS. This should be avoided at all costs.

Monitoring and Evaluation

Introduction of independent evaluation of PS credit is a welcome step. But what is surprising is its understanding of the concepts of monitoring and evaluation. Monitoring is an internal exercise, and evaluation is invariably an external exercise to avoid any bias in studying the implementation aspects of any scheme. Therefore, combining both monitoring and evaluation is improper. Further, it is also desirable that the multiple institutions engaged in such an exercise need not be nationally placed. They can be regionally located institutions having experience in conducting such an evaluation. Further, these studies should also be entrusted to alternate institutions so identified, so that vested interests do not develop. The cost of such studies should be shared between the 3 institutions: the lending bank, the state government, and the central government, in equal proportion. Otherwise, it is not unlikely that the burden of evaluation would be passed on to the borrower over a period of time.

Basel II and Basel III Impacts

The committee is silent on the risk weights and capital provisioning under directed credit portfolio. As such portfolio does not exist in other countries, if it has discussed the implications on the allocated sectors, it would have provided greater confidence to the commercial banks.

Conclusion

In fact, we would suggest the following for appropriate consideration of the committee.

Structural inefficiencies and geographical incongruities cannot be adequately addressed by mere numerical credit allocations to the sectors that have the potential to contribute significantly to the growth of the nation and for poverty alleviation.

1. It is desirable to rechristen the "priority" sectors as strategic sectors so that commercial banks—both Indian and foreign—would give due attention to their commitments and would also include it in their vision and strategy documents with specified roles, from the top management, down to the field staff.
2. Rural credit that has significant component of farm, non-farm and micro-credit should be dispensed mostly in the rural and semi-urban areas. Insisting on commercial banks to perform in rural areas and prove their existence, either by themselves or through their accredited agencies, would alone serve the intended purpose of the committee.
3. Existing institutional mechanism for dispensing credit more meaningfully lies in the cooperative sector which suffers from mismanagement and mis-governance. Both these maladies cannot be addressed adequately with a single package sparsely spread across the nation. We refer to

the Vaidyanathan Committee's package in this regard. 1,07,000 PACS are much more than the rural branches and can be turned into useful economic entities if the state and central governments bring about the needed legislative, managerial, and technological changes to become part of mainstream banking. The Committee failed to send appropriate signals in this regard.

Reference

B. Yerram Raju, 2012, *Inclusion Journal,* January–February, www.skoch.in

WATERSHED MANAGEMENT

CHAPTER 13

Rainfed Farming and Watershed Management

Out of the total geographical area of 328.74 million hectares in the country, 154.5 million hectares are under different crops. But hardly 32 percent of this area gets assured irrigation. The remaining areas are dependent on the monsoon only. The rainfall in such agro-climatic zones is scanty and erratic. NABARD's Annual Report 2011–12 estimates indicate nearly, 65 percent of agriculture is rain-fed and located in resource-poor regions. These regions are home to a majority of small and resource-poor farmers, whose contribution to food and nutrition security has been acknowledged. Therefore, there is a need for greater understanding of rain-fed agriculture and framework for its development.

Only 40 percent of the precipitation makes its way into the soil and recharging the ground water. Seven percent is being stored in different types of harvesting structures (tank, pond, river, reservoir, etc). The remaining water is wasted as evaporation and run off (16.5/35.5 percent) loss, causing serious damage to the soil and environment. It has been estimated that every year, 12,000 million tonnes of top soil, comprising of 8.5 million tonnes of organic matters/nutrients, gets eroded along with run-off water.

The per capita production in our country is quite low compared to others, due to inefficient management of soil and water, which are two main life supporting natural endowments.

Unabated population growth, coupled with exploitation of natural resources like deforestation and over-exploitation of ground water resulted in depletion of soil fertility.

Inefficient land management with traditional methods of cultivation results in low crop yield and affects the productivity of land on long-term basis due to gradual depletion of nutrient levels and soil depth.

What is Dry Land?

Dry land is characterized by low and uncertain rainfall. Based on the average annual rainfall, the entire landmass can be divided into three categories: (a) Low; (b) Medium, and; (c) High, but according to quantum of precipitation, the area can be classified into three agro-climatic zones.

(i) Arid Zone : Rainfall below 500mm
(ii) Semi-Arid Zone : Rainfall between 500 to 750mm
(iii) Humid Zone : Above 750mm

Areas under arid and semi-arid zones are considered as dry lands, which constitute about 67 percent of total cultivable land and contribute 42 percent of total food grain production. Coarse cereals (85 percent), minor millets (95 percent), pulses (90 percent), oil seeds (75 percent) and cotton (70 percent), are the major crops grown in dry land. Nearly, 31 percent of the rural population depends on dry land for earning their livelihood.

Table 13.1: Characteristics of Dry Land

1. Variability in rainfall	7. Low fertilizer intake
2. Undulating topography	8. Low ground water level
3. High soil erosion & depletion	9. Low fertility & productivity
4. Weather aberration	10. High evapo-transpiration
5. Mono cropping	11. High diurnal & annual temperature
6. Low water retention capacity	12. Traditional & sustenance farming-low income

The bulk of rising food demand in the country has to be met by enhancing the productivity of dry land as the productivity of irrigated areas is reaching a plateau. The management of limited water and land resources, involving a multi-disciplinary approach, on devising a most remunerative eco-friendly and environmentally appropriate land use, is the central factor for maximizing crop productivity profitability and sustainability of dry land agriculture.

What is Wasteland?

"Any land, irrespective of ownership, which is producing less than 20 percent of its optimum biological productivity, excepting the current fallow," is called wasteland.

The wasteland is not only confined to known categories like usar, barren, uncultivable/cultivable waste, but also includes all such areas showing serious ailments or limitations, rendering them useless or uneconomic to use to which they are presently put to. The symptoms of ailments may be due to the biotic or natural influences. Presently, 169 million hectares are wasteland, including the degraded forest land.

Characteristics of Wasteland

The land is incapable of producing optimum bio-mass, ecologically unstable and developing toxicity at the root zone of the crops/plants due to salinity/alkalinity of the soil. Other types of wastelands are marine, gullied, marshy lands.

Total cultivable and uncultivable wastelands in our country are 53 million hectares, of which 50 percent are in two states. A large and rapidly growing population in the country, large number of cattle heads, increasing industrialization and urbanization has created tremendous pressure on the land resources which are constant.

Besides low productivity, these wastelands are damaging the national economy by contributing to floods and premature siltation of reservoirs. Wastelands are those degraded lands, which are:

1. Ecologically unsuitable.
2. Where the top soil has developed toxicity in the root zone for the growth of most crops and trees.

Can These Problem Lands be Tackled?

While the demand for food grains is increasing every year due to unabated population growth, and the per capita land availability is shrinking from the level of 0.94 hectare in 1951 to 0.14 hectare in 2000, emphasis has to be laid on rain-fed areas as well as degraded lands to step-up production through technological up-gradation and efficient soil and water management practices.

Planners/research workers, of late, have put serious thought into tackling the problem of food production as well as environmental degradation.

The Government of India appointed a committee in 1994, headed by C. Hanumantayya to suggest solutions to overcome the maladies.

They recommended a set of guidelines common for all the schemes, which are being implemented with effect from 1994–95. The idea is to start with people's movement from the grassroots level, that is the Village. The concept envisages 'watershed approach'. Its core meaning is to involve people in land and water management practices.

Watershed Management

1. Watershed is a pear-shaped undulating land mass where the rain water runs off according to the natural gradient and passes through a common outlet.
2. Watershed is a geo-hydrological/agro-climatic unit, which drain out at a common point from ridge to the valley.
3. It is an upstream area or catchment area of a stream/rivulet/tributary/river.

Watershed Approach is the scientific management of land and water in order to promote the living standard of the people within an identified area, integrating the natural endowments like land, water, vegetation, animal & human being.

Objectives of Watershed Management

1. Prevention of soil erosion from the impact of rain drops.
2. Reducing run-off.
3. Optimum utilization of natural resources.
4. Enriching the soil nutrient level.
5. Tackling obstacles in growth of vegetation.
6. Increase in production (food, fuel, fibre and fodder).
7. Harnessing ground water recharge.
8. Adoption of simple, easy and affordable local technology.
9. Arresting the silting in reservoirs.
10. Sustained community action.
11. Creation of employment.
12. Restoration of ecological balance.
13. Social harmony.

Watershed Project Concept

1. Selection of District/Block: The watershed projects are being implemented in the districts and blocks that have been notified by the Government of India under respective programmes (NWDPRA/DPAP/DDP/IWDP/EAS/IJRY).
2. Selection of Village: Keeping in view the strategy of peoples' participation, selection shall be made where peoples' participation is assured through voluntary donation/contributions (physical/ financial) for the developmental activities as well as for the operation and maintenance of the assets created.
3. Selection of a watershed project: The under noted criteria have been laid down by Government of India along with other requirements discussed in continuation thereto, based on the severity of damages to the land. Willingness of the people living within the eco-space is also taken into consideration. The minimum area of a micro watershed is 500 hectares. The period of implementation is between 4 and 5 years.

Criteria for Selection of Watershed

1. Severity of damage (erosion) to the land.
2. Preponderance of wasteland.
3. At least 50 percent of the area under the watershed is arable.
4. Depleting ground water level.
5. Involvement of poor, including women.
6. Limited scope for irrigation (<30 percent).
7. Preponderance of common land.
8. Acute shortage of drinking water.
9. Presence of SHGs/DWACRA groups.
10. Support from NGOs.

Other information

1. Survey, field investigation and mapping for project preparation (list of supporting data with watershed maps indicating locations).
2. Availability of technical supports for implementation.
3. Crops and cropping pattern to be adopted, input availability, marketing arrangements and communication and infrastructure.

4. Fixing minimum wages and labour-material component ratios (60:40) for implementation of any activity.
5. Formation of Watershed Development Teams (WDTs), SHGs for creating awareness about availability of credit facility for farm and non-farm individual activities.
6. The state government may spell out post-project benefits, on-farm employment generation and impact on area development, as well as on ecology.

Formation of Watershed Sangh/ Watershed Team

A Project Implementation Agency (PIA) need, to be constituted, involving officials from all related government development agencies. NGO are also involved in the programme. PIA undertakes the planning, co-ordination, formulation and implementation of the projects.

The agency will conduct Participatory Rural Appraisal (PRA) exercises to prepare the developmental plans for each watershed, undertake community organization and training for the village communities, and provide technical guidance and supervision of the watershed development activities.

Participatory Rural Appraisal (PRA) Exercise is based on:

1. Resources inventory.
2. Felt needs of the user groups.
3. Present land use pattern & land topography.
4. Optimum use of resources.

Agencies Involved in Watershed Management Projects

1. NWDPRA: National Watershed Development Project for Rain-fed Areas (Ministry of Agriculture).
2. DPAP: Drought Prone Area Programme (Ministry of Rural Development).
3. DDP: Desert Development Programme (Ministry of Rural Development).
4. IWDP: Integrated Wasteland Development (Ministry of Rural Development).
5. EAS: Employment Assurance Scheme (Ministry of Rural Development) 50 percent of the funds now extended to National Rural Employment Guarantee Scheme (NREGS).

6. JIRY: Intensified Jawahar Rojgar Yojana (Ministry of Rural Development) 50 percent of the funds allocated.

The aim of watershed approach in the present context is quite different and aims at not only reducing soil erosion and siltation of reservoirs and river beds but also utilization of water thus stored in the soil, for improving production on the fields of all the farmers whose lands are located in the watershed.

Watershed Development aims at 'Holistic Approach', such as:

1. Conservation and optimum utilization of natural resources, for example, land, water, and vegetation, for sustained productivity.
2. Restoration of ecology by conserving soil, water and greening the area.
3. Increased bio-mass production on a sustained basis.
4. Development of community assets for equitable sharing.
5. Development of human and livestock resources.
6. Improvement of socio-economic conditions of the people.
7. Employment generation during and post project to arrest migration to urban areas.
8. Development of common property resources for the benefit of weaker and landless people.
9. Empowerment of weaker sections and women.

Box 13.1: Watershed Projects Impact—TERI

The Energy & Resources Institute (TERI) prepared a compendium in 2004 which summarizes the major impacts due to the intervention caused by watershed projects in 230 districts of 16 states by independent institutions and bodies. Some of the estimated yields and economic implications as derived by TERI are:

- Overall improvement in land use—Increase in the net sown area, gross cropped area and area sown more than one, Increase in the number of irrigation options in all the areas of watershed projects
- Increase in fuel wood and fodder availability
- An increase in agriculture-related employment opportunities among beneficiaries and in other sectors for non-beneficiaries—Emergence of fishery potential following the development of tanks and other water bodies
- Marked preference for improved breeds after the project.

Watershed Development Project Technological Adoptions

Soil and water conservation methods

1. Preventing the land surface from the impact of raindrops.
2. Increasing infiltration capacity of the soil to reduce run off.
3. Improving the stability of soil aggregates to reduce splash and velocity of runoff water.

Arable lands

Agronomical (biological/ vegetative) measures

1. Suitable cropping pattern and rotation with legume crops.
2. Short-duration, drought-resistant crop varieties.
3. Quality seeds and pest resistant treatment with pesticides (timely sowing with improved implements to ensure proper placement of inputs).
4. Contour cultivation, effective tillage and ploughing the land along the contour, and sowing seeds across the slope where the slope is less than 1.5 percent (will yield more and also reduce erosion).
5. Inter-cropping/mixed cropping (avoids total loss and increases fertility level).
6. Strip cropping, using raising of erosion-permitting and erosion-resisting crops in alternate strips.
7. Conservation tillage/In-situ moisture conservation practices/Inter-bund soil treatments.
8. Mulching (increases microbial activity, infiltration, root distribution and reduces erosion).
9. Intercultural practices (weeding, hoeing, manuring, pest control, etc, bio-pesticides and bio-fertilizer are recommended).

Mechanical/Engineering Measures

1. Contour bunding: Where slope is 5–6 percent (low height earthen barriers to intercept run off and simultaneously increase infiltration).
2. Compartmental bunding: Slope 1.5–5 percent.
3. Graded bunding: Medium and high rainfall areas having low infiltration capacity. This method is adopted to divert excess water where it garners stock through drainage channels at the upstream area of black soil and without channel in red soil (slope between 2–6 percent).

4. Terracing: For hilly areas with slopes more than 10 percent, bench/ step/terracing.
5. Gully control measures.
6. Water conservation/storage structures, including *nallah bunds*, check dams, gully plugs, ponds, percolation tank, etc.
7. Grass waterways/stabilization of *bunds* with grass plantation (khus grass, para grass).
8. Provision of drainage network.
9. Construction of drop structures.

Pasture Development

In places where erosion control by agronomic practices alone, or in combination with mechanical measures, is not possible, and where the land is badly eroded, the best way to put land under grasses/fodders.

For example Napier Rhode, Anjana, Sewan grass, etc., and fodder like Berseem, Lucern, Stylo, Subabul, etc.

Water Harvesting and Recycling

Aims at collection of rain water in a pond and utilizing the same during drought period to give one or two life saving irrigation sessions to the crop. For one hectare of land, a pond measuring 250–300 cubic metres is recommended.

Other Water Harvesting Structures/Measures

Tank, farm pond, dug out, open well, check *bund*, desilting of existing tanks and recharge of wells.

Dry Land Horticulture

Fruit crops like Ber, Custard Apple, Amla, Mango, Guava and Pomegranate are successfully cultivated in dry lands. The returns per unit area from fruit crops are much more than the seasonal grain crops. These crops provide minimum return even during drought years.

Non-arable lands (Alternate Land Use System)

Afforestation in degraded lands.

Social Forestry & Farm Forestry

1. Block plantations with Subabul, Casurina, Eucalyptus, Acacia, Bamboo, Neem, Babul, etc, in degraded lands can supply fuel, fodder and timber.
2. Silvi-Pasture (forest & grass) Bamboo, Eucalyptus, Subabul with grass/ fodder.
3. Medicinal & aromatic plants like Aonla, Sarpagandha, Gugul, Mehandi, Lemongrass, Neem, Senna, Mentha, Aswagandha, Isabgol, Palmarosa, etc., are suitable.

Allied Agriculture Activities

Dairy, piggery, sericulture, goat and sheep rearing and bee keeping are a few examples suitable in dry land areas to supplement the income of farmers.

Cow	Buffalo	Goat	Sheep	Camel
Tharpatker Gir Rathi Sahiwal	Surti Mehsana Jafrabadi	Marwari Jakhrana Kuchchi Osmanabadi Ganjam Sirohi	Marwari Chokla Deccani Sonadi	Bikaneri Jaisalmer

The solution for enhancing production in dry lands ultimately lies in not providing finance for a single activity at a time, but effecting finance for a set package of activities, depending on the requirement of farmer.

Credit Support by Banks

Banks can provide credit to the farmers for the following activities:

1. Working capital/short-term finance like crop loans that is, for purchase of seeds, fertilizers and pesticides.
2. Investment loan/medium-term loan

(a) For purchase of improved version of ploughs, seed drills, seed-cum-fertilizer drills, sprayers, weeders, harvesters and threshers etc.

(b) Land development activities (land levelling, contour bunding, graded bunding, terracing, gully plugging, etc.) Ref Block I, II, and III.

(c) For construction of farm ponds, percolation tank, open well and tube/ bore well, recharging of well, excavation of tank, etc.
(d) For raising of forest crops like eucalyptus, casurina, etc.
(e) For raising of fruit crops like ber, custard apple, phalsa, aonla, tamarind, etc.
(f) For taking up subsidiary occupations like dairy, poultry, sheep/ goat rearing, bee keeping.
(g) Non-farming activities like cottage and village industries.

Advantages to Farmers in Watershed Approach

1. Less cost for the development of land.
2. Reduced soil erosion and fertility loss.
3. Soil and water conservation in situ.
4. Better utilization of natural resources for production purposes.
5. Efficient use of available rainfall.
6. Increased production and higher profits.

Benefits that Accrue to the Society Adopting Watershed Approach

1. Less flood damage to downstream farm land and villages.
2. Reduced siltation of costly irrigation tanks and water reservoirs.
3. Better conservation and development of natural resources.
4. More dependable and clean water supply for domestic and industrial use.
5. Increased availability and supply of foodgrains and industrial raw materials.
6. Increased employment potential.

Common Constraints in Implementation of Watershed Programmes

1. Some farmers do not co-operate with the authorities in taking up soil and water conservation methods upon their lands.
2. Some farmers have already become defaulters to the banks, and hence, lost the eligibility to borrow for implementation of this new technology on their lands.
3. Some farmers, though they cultivate the lands, do not have marketable title to the land to offer it as a security for term loans.

NABARD's Initiative

Participatory watershed development projects, with the aim of enhancing productivity and profitability of rain fed agriculture in a sustainable manner, have been funded by NABARD from a corpus that initially started at Rs 200 crore in 1999–2000 to Rs 1,806.03 crore at the end of March 2012. It anchors 4 watershed development programmes in the country, covering over 1.78 million hectares. These programmes are: Indo-German Watershed Development Programme (IGWDP) in Maharashtra, Andhra Pradesh, Gujarat and Rajasthan; Participatory Watershed Development Programme under Watershed Development Fund in 15 states; Prime Minister's package for distressed districts in 4 states and; Integrated Watershed Development Programme (IWDP) in Bihar, supported by the Planning Commission.

NABARD periodically conducts evaluation of its projects from independent agencies and a few of its findings reported in its Annual Report would be in order.

Impact Evaluation Findings of Watershed Projects (2011)

(a) Kannamangala Watershed, Chickballapur District in Karnataka between 2002 and 2009, cropped area (Rabi) increased from 157 hectares to 443 hectares (182% increase), orchards from 88 hectares to 149 hectares, wastelands reduced from 85 hectares to 35 hectares and fallow land reduced by 485 hectares. There was no decline in the water table.

(b) Midcourse Impact of Four IGWDP watersheds in Andhra Pradesh:
- There was employment generation of 73,217 person days.
- Water storage capacity stood at 35,114 cm
- Crops which registered higher productivity levels were cotton (32%) and vegetables (29%) in Laksmipur watershed; cotton (38%) and red gram (35%) in Shivarvenkatpur; cotton red gram (153%), maize (11%) and Kharif paddy (31%) in Kakatiya watershed and cotton (34%), wheat (34%) and Kharif paddy (32%) in Shettihadapnur.

Among the watersheds, the real income change was highest (48%) in Shettihadapnur watershed, followed by Kakatiya (40%), Lakshmipur (15%), Shivarvenkatpur (13%).

The extent of migration has reduced in all the four watersheds. The level of reduction was the highest in Kakatiya (52%), followed by Shettihadapnur (35%), Laksmipur (35%) and Shivrvenkatpur (22%).

Source: NABARD Annual Report 2011-12.

AGRICULTURAL MARKETING AND ORGANIZED RETAIL TRADE

CHAPTER 14

Financing Farmers for Agricultural Marketing

A huge gap needs to be met for post-harvest operations sans processing viewed in the context of the recommendations of the Agricultural Credit Review Committee (Khusro Committee). Even this committee estimated marketing credit only for private traders. Farming is not viewed as an extended enterprise. An industry is an enterprise, where from production to sale, the industrialist secures credit at every stage, while for the farmer, credit is restricted only for production. A propensity appraisal system of farmer's credit requirements has been suggested.

With increase in agricultural production, forward linkages, such as (a) agro-processing industries (b) storage, transportation, marketing, and export of agricultural produce, will have to be strengthened to enable farmers to realize remunerative prices for the increased produce.[1] The agro-processing industries can be grouped under 3 broad heads: (a) crop production; (b) wood, and; (c) livestock. Agro-processing for crop production can again be sub-divided into 6 main heads: (a) foodgrains; (b) oil seeds; (c) fruits and vegetables; (d) sugarcane; (e) fibre crops, and; (f) plantation crops. Agricultural produce marketing is the focus in this chapter.

According to the report on Currency and Finance, RBI, 1997–8, total direct institutional finance for agriculture and allied activities during the Eighth Five Year Plan (1992–1997) increased from Rs. 11,199 crores in the beginning of 1992–93 to Rs 25,498.70 crores at the end of 1996–97 at an annual compound growth rate of 17.90 percent. Impressive as it may look, there has been a decline in the credit disbursed during the year 1996–97 just Rs 2,210.8 crores by all the institutions, namely, commercial banks, cooperative banks, RRBs and state governments.

Table 14.1 Scheduled Commercial Banks' Outstanding Advances Against Select Commodities

(Rs Crores)

		March 1997		March 1998	
		Amt.	Percentage	Amt.	Percentage
1.	Food Grains	1,557.2	28.5	2,242.8	31.9
2.	Sugar	1,586.9	29.0	2,294.0	32.6
3.	Major Oil Seeds	467.5	8.6	504.3	7.2
4.	Major Veg. Oils	515.2	9.4	587.6	8.4
5.	Cotton & Kapas	1,204.9	22	1,268.3	18.0
6.	Raw Jute	134.9	2.5	130.3	1.9
	Total	5,466.7	100.0	7,027.4	100.0

This excludes advances to Cotton Corporation of India, Jute Corporation of India and NDDB.

The purpose-wise investment credit disbursements by NABARD during 1997–98 indicated a loan outflow of just Rs 14 crores (0.4 percent) of the total of Rs 3,922 crore for marketing, same as that in the previous year, and a decline from Rs 21 crores in 1995–96.

NCDC's disbursements for processing, marketing and storage activities declined from Rs 363 crores in 1995–96 to Rs 323.70 crores in 1997–98. Food grain production (rice, wheat, coarse cereals and pulses) during the year 1996–97 was 199.3 metric tonnes. Sugarcane production was of the order of 277.3 metric tonnes, Tobacco 0.6 metric tonnes, Jute and Mesta 11.0 million bales of 180 kg each, cotton 14.3 million bales of 170 kg each, 25 million tonnes of oil seeds during the same year. Whether we look at the volume of credit for marketing from the point of view of total credit for agriculture or production, it is negligible.

Rs 25,498.7 crores disbursements under direct institutional finance for agriculture at current prices fall short of the estimated demand for credit (Khusro Committee) at 1984–85 prices at Rs 30,804 crores.

Table 14.2: Khusro Committee Estimated Financial Requirements for Storage

Commodities	Stocking '000 metric tonnes	Financial Requirements (Rs Cr.)	Credit Requirements (Rs Cr.)
Wheat	9,336	3,913	326
Rice	10,451	10,451	871
Pulses	2,222	2,291	191
Other Cereals	3,036	1,408	117
Total	25,045	18,063	1,505

Credit requirements for storage capacity at 1984–85 prices, as estimated by the committee for these commodities, was Rs 593 crores by the year 1999–2000. At the margins prevailing in 1984–85, the Khusro Committee estimated short-term credit for storage of grains at Rs 4,202 crores and for construction of storage godowns, at Rs 593 crores. The committee has assumed increase in credit requirements at 5 percent per annum on account of increase in prices. Accordingly, both short-term and long-term credit for marketing, storage and transportation have been placed at Rs 9,981 crores at 1984–85 prices, by the year 1999–2000. At current prices, it would be Rs 26,754 crores against this estimate. Even after the commission on agricultural costs and prices raised the base prices of food grains steeply, the actual disbursals at current prices did not cross Rs 950 crores by 1996–97. It is obvious that the gap would not be made up by all the lending institutions together.

When the financing institutions think of marketing as an activity, they should consider all the marketing tasks and responsibilities which may be summarized as follows:

1. Finding a buyer and transferring ownership.
2. Assembling and storing.
3. Sorting, packing and processing.
4. Assorting and presenting to consumers.
5. Providing the finance for marketing and risk-taking[2].
6. Advertisement and branding.

The financing institution should realise that marketing enables the farmer to move from semi-substance to growing produce regularly for sale. An efficient marketing sector, which will play a dynamic role in stimulating output and consumption, is the most important multiplier of economic development. These markets are currently in four broad categories:

1. Independent, locally based private firms.
2. Cooperatives or farmers' associations.
3. Marketing boards, State Trading Corporations and officially sponsored development agencies.
4. Transnational companies with access to processing technologies and external markets.

Financing agricultural marketing by the banking system is mostly by way of term loans to a trading intermediary: (a) for construction of storage godowns; (b) for construction of market yards, and; (c) for construction of cold storages.

A few banks have financed the farmers' short-term working capital against warehouse receipts of central/state warehousing corporations. We have noticed that the total sum of such loans works out to barely Rs 14–20 crores! It will be ludicrous to calculate the percentage to the total value of production.

The second category of marketing finance is for exports of agricultural products—rice, wheat, floriculture, horticulture products, etc.—to agri-business houses and agro-industry. In respect to crops like tobacco, turmeric, etc, a few farmers also received credit for storage until the markets commenced operations during the season. Some traders in these commodities secured finance in these commodities both on open book positions (demand over the sale proceeds) and on consignment basis.

The Indian farmer is not viewed as an extended enterprise. Every salaried employee is a preferred borrower to the farmer and every salaried person contracts loans for a multiplicity of purposes: (a) for buying consumer goods; (b) for building a house; (c) for equipping a house; (d) against his savings, like PF, Insurance; (e) against the shares; (f) against pledge of gold ornaments and; (g) for purchase of a vehicle, and sometimes against even his creditors! Although the RBI guidelines stipulate that a farmer can be granted credit for storage for a period of three to four months of his own grain to secure a better price, not many banks have encouraged this and a limit of Rs 50,000, per person without the applicability of selective credit controls, but with relationship to production credit, is a reasonable limit that would have made every farmer happy, and the banks happy as well with least NPAs. 70 percent of the economy is dependent on agriculture, and its contribution to the NPAs is just 7 percent of the total. If there are no political write-offs of principal/ interest, the NPAs would have been still less.

The KCC introduced very recently by a few public sector banks at the instance of Government of India and the NABARD, is just a beginning to meeting the input costs of cultivation and consumption requirements at a more comprehensive level. At the farmers' meet organised by the Government of Andhra Pradesh from March 19 to 22 and a parallel meeting of farmers organised by the Bharatiya Kisan Sangh, not even a single farmer received the credit card so far from any bank.

In the first decade of agricultural finance by the banks, they encouraged tie-up arrangements with the processing industries tobacco crop financing with tobacco industry (VST, ILTD, etc.), sugarcane crop with sugar factories in the private and cooperative sectors, etc. and some arrangements continue even till date. Loan recovery is affected through the intermediary for such arrangements. Since these are commercial crops carrying high volume of credit, such intermediation arrangements obviously reduced the financing risks to the barest minimum. With respect to a few fruit crops like Litchi, Grapes etc, which had export potential, as referred to earlier, open book options and consignment financing was taken up. Such intermediation was considered infeasible with respect to food crops like rice, wheat, etc.

This clearly shows that the banks went in more for least risk routes. Even with respect to crops, they had lent mostly in irrigated areas. 88 percent of their crop finance is restricted to just 10 states in the country. Still, they ended up with 7 percent as NPAs because they had lent without proper appreciation of the farmer's and crop's requirements.

Propensity Appraisal System

Credit to farmer, if worked out on his propensity to consume, that is, backwards from his cashing, in capacity, the farmer would have been assisted more purposively and productively by the banking system. The Propensity Appraisal System (PAS) of farm credit is linked to the calendar of asset creation by the farmer. The crop asset on the field, asset-in-harvest, storage, cash realization (financial asset), would all require assistance from the lender.

The risks that are attendant on such asset financing, stem from the following:

1. Seasonality of the crop and the consequent price fluctuations.
2. Shelf life of the products/produce.
3. Storage (losses caused by rodent, wastage, handling, loss of weight due to the drying up of grain, etc.).
4. Transport.

There are in-built costs of carrying the assets. Some of these risks need to be hedged by the banker through interest rates and other cost recovery mechanisms.

Many farmers, who are on mono- or double-cropping, have a tendency to fall back on one season's output for the family's consumption requirements while credit is availed for all seasons and all crops. A banker who plans for recovery from the cash-in-season/crops, would be getting 100 percent recovery. At least, this is my personal experience. If these farmers are helped to store their grains, they will be more grateful to the bank, and again, recovery will be 100 percent. A farmer, who sells grain wet, gets less price for more weight—a double loss. He cannot but do this if he has no means of storing and selling at a later date. A grain stored, loses weight, become qualitatively superior, and secures higher price. The same is not true in the case of crops like tobacco, cotton or chillies, where de-colouring beyond the optimum storage time diminishes the quality and gets less price for less weight/volume. Unfortunately, the Kinship effect in cropping is so high that if a farmer raises a particular crop due to an announced higher crop price, all the others follow. This leads to increased production, glut in the market and low price. The initial assumptions involved in the farmer selecting a particular crop against his interests. In fact, some of the tobacco companies, under tie-up arrangements, encouraged farmers to go in for white barley, and Virginia tobacco crops, promising a fair rate, and the farmers fell for the offer. The companies ensured the proper cultural practices through extension efforts. When the bumper crop was realized, they bought the whole crop in the first year. In the second year, although a similar bumper crop was realized, the tobacco companies did not pick up the crop or picked up late. The late pick-up led to the "golden" tobacco becoming "brass" tobacco, diminishing its value. The loss to the farmer, as a result, could not be compensated. But banks realized the loans due to the tie-up arrangement. The farmers' switch over to other crops is not like switching on a light. Alternate cropping pattern through vigorous extension efforts are very necessary to ensure that the forward linkages become remunerative to the farmer.

Therefore, if the farmer is appraised for his credit facilities backwards, from his propensity to consume and the propinquity to save for a rainy day and repay, the prospects of the entire farm credit system becoming more productive, are bright.

The duration for which market finance should be made available is again dependent on the price volatility. Both the type of the product/produce (as discussed earlier) and the quantum of loan, have a bearing on the repayment behaviour of the farmer. There should be a maturity match to the price volatility.

Suppose that the end price of a product is x. The recovery should be programmed as follows:

(0.6x)x at 60%	-	20%
(0.8x)x at 80%	-	20%
(x)x at 100%	-	60%

If the schedule of recovery thus corresponds to price volatility, the farmer would not find it difficult to respond to the financing system. While it is not desirable to extend subsidies, which have made the farmer a beggar, there should be safety nets or social policy premium built into the state government budgets. Rytu Bazars, a modest start, are a pointer to such interventions where the government has provided for transport of vegetables and fruits to the selling venue and social amenities there at.

Therefore, a few questions that demand an answer are:

1. When we talk of finance for storage and marketing, are we talking of farmers or traders?
2. If it is for traders, why should we worry about it in this forum?
3. If it is for the farmer what are the factors that contributed to such low volumes of credit and how can they be remedied?

We have seen the issues relating to the farmer.

Unlike in the manufacturing sector, where every producer will be a cash seller throughout the period of production, in the farm sector, every farmer will end up as producer and consumer, and not a seller, because all that is produced will not be sold even with a reasonable time gap between production and sale. Secondly, if the trader does not get credit for procurement and storage, the produce is retained with the farmer. Therefore, the trader becomes an important intermediary between the producing farmer and retail consumer. This is the reason for Khusro Committee assessing the financial requirements of the private wholesale trade in food grains, taking into consideration the movement of food grains from their arrival into the wholesale market to the point of reaching the retail consumer and for export. Further, every producing farmer is more a net consumer from the system than a mere producer, while every trader is a net trader. Every farm produce needs value addition before consumption. What needs to be financed, and who needs to be financed—one must be clear about this.

The costs incurred at the trading point would be:

1. Purchase price of the produce.
2. Handling, grading.
3. Packaging.
4. Transporting.
5. Storage, etc.

Very scanty data is available regarding the marketing prices and costs. While traders deal in a variety of commodities, the farmer produces very few, most often, two to three, except when he takes up mixed farming.

The storage capacity and proper transportation facilities are key determinants in the ultimate price to the producer. The storage technology was not within the reach of the small farmer, whose tradeable surpluses are also small. Even where adequate guidelines provided for financial assistance to silos and small storage godowns, the banks did not put these schemes on their showcase for fear of greater work and higher credit volumes to the agricultural sector.

The World Bank Storage Godown Project, financed through the cooperative banks, NDDB, NCDC, etc, did not result in creation of storage capacity acceptable to the producer from the points of view of reach and cost. Most of them are abandoned.

The cold storage is mostly in the private sector, financed by the State Finance Corporations and banks. Farmers from Hindupur come to Vijayawada and Guntur, to store their tamarind and chillies, because the wholesale market is close. Banks do not finance the cold storage receipts on par with the state/ central warehouse receipts, although both are on par in so far as risk factors are concerned.

Role of the State

The state continues to play a very important role in the structural aspects of agricultural markets. They broadly relate to (a) development and regulation of primary markets, and; (b) regulation of market conduct through a series of legal instruments. The former is based covered under Regulated Markets while the latter is covered by a few legal instruments apart from the state enactments relating to produce markets.

1. Agricultural Produce (Grading and Marking) Act.
2. Prevention of Food Adulteration Act, 1954, 1964, 1976, 1986.
3. Essential Commodities Act, 1955.
4. Solvent Extracted Oil, De-oiled Meal and Edible Oil (Control) Order, 1967.
5. Meat Food Products Order, 1973.
6. Standards of Weights and Measures Act, 1976.
7. Pulses, Edible Oil Seeds and Edible Oils Storage Control Order, 1977.
8. Vegetable Oil Products (Control) Order, 1977.
9. Prevention of Black Marketing and Maintenance of Supply of Essential Commodities Act, 1980.
10. The Cold Storage Order, 1964, 1980 (rescinded in 1997).
11. Consumer Protection Act, 1986.
12. Bureau of Indian Standard Act, 1986.
13. Milk and Milk Products Order, 1992.
14. Fruit Products Order, 1955, 1997.

The provisions under the legal instruments, most being consumer protection measures, are used to regulate the activities of traders and processors pertaining to trading, stocking, maintenance of quality, grading, packing, processing, blending and movements. The future trading in agricultural commodities is also regulated by the government.[3]

The financing institutions which lend against the primary security of stocks run the risk of non-compliance of the provisions of so many Acts by their borrowers. Since the penal provisions for non-compliance are administered by the respective regulatory authorities, the lender may not even know till a news item appears or a noise is made, that the primary security has been taken possession of. Lender does not have are course unless he collaterally secures such stocks. If farmers are provided the marketing finance, they get into the shoes of a trader until the stocks are sold. The financing institution does not know the legal implications of financing marketing activity. Therefore, I would suggest that NABARD brings out a compendium of such implications and the aspects that the banker should take note of during the course of monitoring such advances. Ignorance of law cannot be accepted as an excuse and the vicarious provisions of disciplinary action on the unintended provisions errors/omissions will be applied when the banks incur financial loss as a consequence, to the officials manning these advances. A secure environment for lending is very important and it needs to be created by the apex financing institution.

Economic liberalization can be expected to result in an increase in requests for aid for agricultural markets. Indian regulated market laws over specifies conduct. It is a highly ideological law stipulating that one contractual form is efficient. "The law needs to be reformed so as to state what is unacceptable conduct, thereby freeing a larger legitimate contractual space."[5]

Enforcement has to be standardized and powerful, and at the same time should have positive incentives for compliance. This would facilitate farmers converting their form steads into viable enterprises, eligible for financing on their own merit.

Market places tend towards specification, for example, Anakapalle (AP) for jaggery, Guntur (AP), Palladam (Tamil Nadu) and Koduvai (Tamil Nadu) for Tobacco, Adoni (AP), Guntakal (AP) and Tirupur (Tamil Nadu), for cotton, Avanashi (Tamil Nadu) for grain, etc. They are enthusiastically welcomed as growth poles, benefiting from agglomeration economies derived from special infrastructure provision, concentration of the kind of information which facilitates innovation and market access via collective representation.[4] Such clusters have always attracted the attention of bankers because of the availability of cross functional information, which itself acts as insurance for the risk capital.

When it comes to the question of financing diversified markets situated sometimes away from the hinterland of general financing activity, the field staff should have some appraisal system hands-on. A typical information layout is furnished in the annexure.

Financing marketing activity in the Agricultural sector is as complex and varied as agricultural activity itself, with a large number of buyers and sellers associated with imperfections in market information and myriad regulatory instruments. All the regulatory laws should be consolidated into an Act. A compendium for compliance should be prepared in the mean time by NABARD to act as a guide. Propensity Appraisal System should be introduced to finance the farmer when the calendar of assets in various forms resting with farmer, could be lent safely.

Notes

1. ACRC, 1987.
2. John C. Abbott, 1987, *Agricultural Marketing Enterprises for the Developing World*, Cambridge University Press.
3. S.S. Acharya, "Agricultural Marketing: Issues and Challenges", *Indian Journal of Agricultural Economics*, Vol. 53(3), p. 98.
4. K. Nadri, H. Schmitz, 1994, "Industrial clusters in less Developed Countries: Review of Experiences and Research Agenda", Discussion Paper 339, Institute of Development Studies, University of Sussex.
5. Barbara Harriss-White, 1996, *A Political Economy of Agricultural Markets in South India,* pp. 307–337, 341.

References

S.S. Acharya, "Agricultural Marketing: Issues and Challenges", *Indian Journal of Agricultural Economics*, Vol. 53(3), pp. 311–13.

Jagadish Prasad and Arabind Prasad, 1995, (ed), *Indian Agricultural marketing, Emerging Trends and Perspectives*, Mittall Publications.

B. Yerram Raju, 1987, Agricultural Credit Review Committee, RBI, pp. 881–923.

Raju, 1997–98, Currency and Finance, Mumbai, RBI, Vol. I, Vols 13 to 45.

Raju, 1998, PROBITY, Mumbai, October, Ch. 3 pp. 3–1 to 3–2.

CHAPTER 15

Organized Retailing and Farm Economy: FDI Retail is No Threat to the Indian Farmer

A number of studies had derided the change, adding to the millions of gigabytes on FDI reform package of UPA2. When one goes into the fine print and analysis, a faulty design and biased sample in those studies stares at us. Thus far, we had misplaced priorities and misdirected investments in the farm sector. The sector has 8 Ministries at the centre, and at least 4 Ministries in the state governments and agriculture markets are governed by at least 9 regulatory Acts and Orders that continue to keep the farmer in distress. A country anxious to usher in reforms, ostensibly to benefit the farmer, has to first address coordination issues and seek solutions in information and communication technologies.

My micro study in urban and metro areas, where the E-Chouppal, MORE, Reliance, Heritage and the like opened mega retail malls, revealed that during the last 3 years, in their periphery, a minimum of 4 and a maximum of 10 small *kirana* shops and retail stores started functioning. While the mega retail stores are attracting persons with brand-goers, the large number of retailers continues to serve consumers of lower means and those buying on credit. These small businesses buy on credit and sell on credit, sans any commercial bank lending to them. There is no history of any such retail stores winding up during the last ten years. More particularly, in the rural areas, farmer consumers buy their requirements on credit and such credit would not certainly come forth from the organized retail and FDI malls that might get entry, albeit within boundaries of policy interventions announced.

It is not the farmer who failed the economy, but it is the economy that failed the farmer. It failed to assure minimum price (cost plus) to the farmer right after sale, that too, in cash. This 'cash' that he gets only in season has to meet household consumption for the whole year, loan repayments both for production and social purposes, asset purchases and margins on future investments. Hence, Agricultural Markets Yards (AMYs) in the farm sector have a crucial positive role that belied all hopes thus far. They need restructuring.

Sixty-five percent of agricultural produce continues to be locally disposed of in respect of food grains and cereals through the dominant private trader—moneylender. Future investments should therefore move into the AMYs suffering from inadequate and unscientific storage facilities, as also unregulated payments and settlement systems. The existing AMPC Act 2005 needs a thorough modification to make farmer-friendly investments. Here is the recipe.

Most Recent Study of CII (2012)

The report, titled "*Emerging Consumer Demand: Rise of the Small Indian Town*" said that 42 of 83 categories in small towns or middle India grew at least 10 percent in same-store sales (differential in revenue generated by a retail chain's existing outlets over a certain period).

The report noted that the small town population wanted to shop like the metros. Evolved FMCG categories such as pre-post wash, hair conditioners, air fresheners and cheese, appear to have topped consumer demand in small towns. The report further added that the total number of stores in small towns rose from 8.23 lakh in June 2008 to 9.26 lakh in May 2011, an average addition of over 250 stores per town.

Expansion Spree

The top ten FMCG players have aggressively expanded in towns with a population of 1 to 10 lakh, adding 29,892 stores on an average in the last year alone. This translates to an increased supply infrastructure, which in turn appears to have helped marketers push products to consumers faster. Marketers who have recognised the potential and invested in these regions a few years ago are reaping rich dividends today, the study added.

However, apart from changing business models and strategies, marketers need to cultivate their brands and keep a constant check on changing consumption patterns. "Retailers and other players need to understand that the big hypermarkets and large malls will not work in a small town. Also, they should focus on issues relating to the needs and importance of consumers, the manner in which demand is picking up, and the importance of marketing strategies that respond to the changing and dynamic consumer demands unique to India," the report added. High GDP growth, disposable income and a young demography are driving the Indian consumption story. It is worthwhile to recall what Rahul Bajaj, Chairman, Bajaj Auto Ltd, said: "Our marketing strategies have to grasp our own realities. Success today hinges on the ability to anticipate, or better still, to create a future. Who better to influence it than marketing people, who are closest to the market place?" Contextual or circumstantial evidence leaves much to be desired to improve the infrastructure for agriculture markets, where FMCG originates.

Facilities at Market Yards should be Comprehensive

Market yard boundary; auction platform; shops; godowns; cattleshed; water huts; rest house; dormitories; public lavatory; water troughs for cattle; public urinals; bank; post office; canteen; weighbridge; warehouse; covered shed; tower light; street lights; genset for alternate power supply; cooperative marketing society; grading and packing facilities must exist for purposes of value addition to the farmer.

Governance

Agricultural Market Yards' Boards of Management should largely represent the farmers instead of traders, and should be the body to decide on a host of areas through a number of professional committees: Recruitment Committee; Audit Committee; Risk Management Committee; Investment Committee; Grievance Redressal Committee, etc, with qualified professionals provided for in the 97th Amendment to the Constitution Act of 2011, who would guide their effective functioning, but outside the purview of voting for all resolutions passed by the Board. The Board thus is the centre of gravity for decision making.

We have permitted multi-commodity exchanges ahead of creating spot markets that held up price discovery mechanisms for the farmer. If the spot markets come up at AMYs, the threshold of farmers' entry, it can resolve many issues. These require huge investments that can now be facilitated by the FDIs.

Each market yard has to computerize its operations, right from the entry of the farmer with his produce into the market. Each farmer getting produce to the Yard can be given a biometric SMART card linked to Aadhar. Once the farmer swipes the SMART card at the gate, it should record simultaneously the stated quantity of the produce brought in by him, verified with the laden weight of the mode of transport. It also records the handling, *hamali* and weighment charges payable by him on the declared quantity. Depending on the arrival time, the farmer gets an entry pass into the dormitory or lodging facility for overnight stay by means of a dormitory coupon, the charges for which would be deducted from the payment for the produce he delivers. The produce brought will be given a bin card and it is unloaded and kept at the weighing platform linked to a computer. The computerized record of the weighment passes on through the network, to the grading chamber where the produce moves to. After grading, the second weighment takes place in accordance with the grades and the prices determined on the trading or auction platform. This information again moves through the network to the packing department. The graded produce appropriately gets packed, and computerized labelling takes place. Then it moves to the cash counter where the farmer, on production of the SMART card, gets the payment after deducting all the service charges, and can even get it credited to his bank account instantaneously through NEFT. All the charges deducted for various services should be as displayed on the tariff board for the services. No farmer is allowed to pay in cash for any service including that for the *hamalis*. The payment for *hamalis* would be settled by the AMY at such intervals as agreed upon between them and the AMY. The *hamalis* should also be covered under the existing social security systems for unorganized workers.

Alternatively, the farmer wanting to sell produce at a future date goes to spot exchange located in the same premises fed with the data of the farmer's arrivals, he would opt for storing in the accredited warehouse or cold storage in the same yard or close-by, to obtain credit by pledging the warehouse receipt to the extent of 75 percent of the market price of the quantity stored, after deducting the charges for storage. If the actual realization falls short of the predetermined future price date, the actual market price, he would get the price at which he stored the price. Grain stored is weight lost and price gained. Stocks have to be insured at the cost of the farmer if they are large and medium, and the state if they are small and marginal. Small and marginal farmers should be provided the pre-declared subvention for insurance and credit and such payment by the state should be online by the Department of Agriculture into the claimant's account with the bank concerned.

FDIs in retail can projectize all such investments that have immense potential to change the farm economy, with no need for farm loan waivers that have axed discipline in lending, in the name of equity. There is enough space for small businesses and organized retailers, once FDIs are calibrated to deliver value to the farmer.

Presentation at the seminar on "Organized Retailing and Farm Economy" by the Indian Society of Agriculture Marketing in October 2012.

CHAPTER 16

Risk Management in Agriculture

Farmers are exposed to risks arising from rainfall variability, market price fluctuations, credit uncertainty, and adoption of new technology. In other words, the farmers basically face weather risk, product risk, price risk and market risk. The diversities in the sources of risks require a variety of instruments for protecting farmers. In India, these include crop insurance, rainfall insurance, farm income insurance and a calamity relief fund. Most of these measures, other than crop insurance, are in the experimental stage. The farmer is pretty unsure of the product because of uncertainty in the quality of the seed he purchased at the time of sowing. There are states where the State Seed Act is in position with varying degrees of regulatory imperfections and implementation failures. Still, the farmer gambles with his sweat. The quantity targeted for production is at best a guesstimate. The marketable surplus for most small and marginal farmers is again, uncertain. Neither the farmer nor the extension machinery has farm planning as an integral part of farm future. Even where it existed, the farmer does not swear by it. After the produce comes to hand and after arriving at the marketable surplus, the farmer is also unsure of the price, whether it fetches him cost of inputs plus a reasonable margin for maintenance, excepting for a few cereal crops where state subvention exists. These uncertainties cast their shadow on the policy approaches and implementation agenda of the credit institutions.

Vyas Committee (2005) and the internal working group on agricultural credit of the RBI have identified a majority of the problems and modified directions to the banks for ensuring enhanced credit flow to agriculture. But would it mitigate the inherent risks and provide adequate insurance to the lender? This remains an unanswered question. If credit for agriculture is a commercial proposition, banks would flock to it. Unfortunately, it is not. The efforts to make it viable and bankable through the supposedly cost-effective interventions like correspondents, agents, and contract farming route, are in the nascent stage. In the meantime, distress of farmers is reflected sadly in suicides in a few stressed regions like Andhra Pradesh, Maharashtra, Karnataka, Punjab, etc. The package announced by the Prime Minister in 2006 is reportedly yet to reach in full measure. Banks are in the throes of implementing Basel II that adds a new dimension to examining risks attached to financing agriculture from the point of view of capital adequacy. Except corporate lending for agriculture, all other farm lending remains away from the cover of either tangible security or sovereign guarantee, and thus, also away from external rating institutions. Unrated and unsecured credit carries higher capital allocation (of course, the regulator is considerate in providing 75 percent CRAR for the present). However, in the context of global presence of a few banks that also carry a reasonably large portfolio of farm credit—at 18 percent of the total credit to go for agriculture—how long this concessionary platform would be available for is a question mark. This paper intends to examine the risk mitigation efforts in the farm sector and see whether enough enthusiasm can be generated among the credit agencies to take to farm lending as a fish takes to water, in the context of Basel II.

Figure 16.1: Cycle of Risk Management

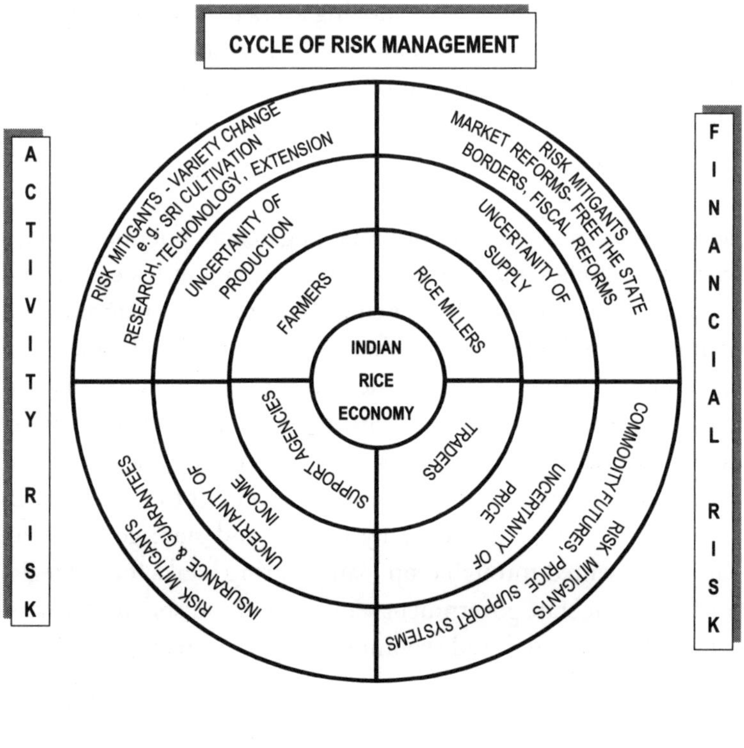

The financial insecurity thus arises from the weak links in the value chain of most farm products, notwithstanding the sporadic interventions of ITC, MSSRF, commodity futures, SHG women groups resorting to market operations in a few districts successfully in Andhra Pradesh, etc. Financial efficiency at the farm front may be improved predominantly in two ways: cost cutting and better realization. One is internal and the other is external and is subject to market fluctuations. However much the farmer would like to cut costs through appropriate technology interventions, labour costs continue to rise providing serious limitations on internal efficiencies. External factors influencing efficiency are market related, and therefore, the need for state subvention, both through insurance and guarantee mechanisms, hardly requires emphasis. Let me attempt a review of their performance.

Risk Mitigation Efforts

Crop Insurance

The NAIS, introduced in Rabi 1999–2000, and implemented by the Agricultural Insurance Corporation (AIC) is a major public sector initiative to mitigate yield risk. The yield loss assessment is based on 'threshold yield' and 'level of indemnity'. The threshold yield is the 3 year moving average yield for rice and wheat and 5 years moving average for other crops. The unit area for assessing the actual yield has been district and the indemnity levels fixed at 90 percent, 80 percent and 60 percent for compensation under the scheme based on crop cutting experiments. The schemes cover a wide range of crops, including food crops (cereals, millets and pulses), oil seeds and annual commercial/horticulture crops in respect of which past data on yield are available for a sufficient number of years. Sugarcane, potato, cotton, ginger, onion, turmeric, chillies, pineapple, banana, jute, coriander, cumin and garlic have also been covered under this scheme. The entire loan amount is insured at a premium rate of 3.5 percent for kharif bajra and oil seeds, and 2.5 percent for other crops, or actuarial rates, if the above rates are higher than actuarial rates. Small and marginal farmers are entitled to 10 percent premium subsidy, which is shared equally by central and state governments. The rates are uniform across states. The claims over and above 100 percent of the premium amount, and administrative costs, are borne by central and state governments. The scheme is implemented through crop loan granting banks for the regions and crops notified by the state governments, and are compulsory for farmers taking a crop loan from banks and voluntary for non bank loaners. During

1999–2010, the premium collected was Rs 6,302.7 crore per annum; the subsidy was Rs 765.89 crore per annum and the total claim was Rs 20,395.08 crore per annum, implying an expenditure of about Rs 1,000 crore per annum by central and state governments over and above the administrative costs incurred by AIC.[1] The claim-premium ratio was high at 3.23 for all the crops; and 6.77 for crops such as groundnut.

The NAIS covered only about 13.6 percent of the cropped area. Moreover, there are significant disparities in insurance coverage across crops and states. Groundnut accounted for 36 percent of claims whereas crops such as maize and jowar accounted for less than 2 percent of claims each, and among the states, Gujarat alone accounted for more than 15.31 percent of total claims, whereas Goa, Haryana and Jammu and Kashmir accounted for less than 1 percent each. Even with 10 percent of coverage of cropped area, excluding the administrative costs, the scheme would have cost central and state governments together Rs 1,000 crore if all claims were met. Some of the weaknesses can be attributed to adverse selection and moral hazard problems (the crop shown as cultivated in record is different from the crop that is actually lost on account of calamity. There is connivance of the farmer and the banker in quite a few instances). High premium rates (for example, as high as 8 percent for cotton and 10 percent for banana crop in Andhra Pradesh), collusion between implementing agencies and farmers in wrongful claims and ignorance of warranty conditions of the policies, led to inefficiencies. The policy of charging uniform rates across states without taking into consideration risks peculiar to the area where the crop is sown, and the risk-sharing mechanism between the insurer and lender, deserve a relook.

The central government launched the Farm Income Insurance Scheme (FIIS) on a pilot basis in 20 districts during Rabi 2003–04 for rice and wheat. The farmer will be paid the difference between actual income and guaranteed crop income per hectare. The guaranteed income is obtained by valuing threshold yield at the minimum support price fixed by the central government and the actual income by valuing actual yield at the prevailing market price. District is the unit of area for yield considerations. The central government meets the expenditure in excess of the premium amounts as well as the administration costs incurred in operating the scheme.

Field visits and empirical studies reveal the poor performance of existing schemes. The insurance coverage of NAIS is very little and its spread is mostly limited to a few states; insurance cover is not available to crops like fruits and vegetables; and there is inordinate delay in the settlement of claims. The indemnity level of 60 percent is very low and needs to be increased[2]. There is demand for making gram panchayat the threshold area, basing premium rates on actuarial rates and subsidy at half the premium rate. Marginal and small farmers may be requiring higher rates of subsidy. This requires a substantial increase in the number of crop-cutting experiments, substantial financial resources and trained manpower. 'In the case of rainfall insurance, although the moral hazard problem may not exist, its efficacy is conditional on yield predicting power of the rainfall index, which is likely to depend on soil conditions, irrigation level and crops among others.' Research on comparative evaluation of crop insurance, rainfall insurance and insurance based vegetation stress indices is needed. The system of SHG-based insurance to manage a part of the risk at the village level also requires scrutiny.

Disaster Mitigation

The National Calamity Contingency Fund (NCCF) created by the central government deals with severe calamities and meets the excess over and above the balance available in the state's calamity relief fund. The Twelfth Finance Commission has recommended that implementation of NAIS should be a precondition for assistance from NCCF. It is desirable that this Fund is managed by NABARD with contribution to the Fund by the state and central governments, participating banks and RRBs, albeit nominally.

Weather Risk and Drought Mitigation

The AIC introduced *Varsha Bima* as a pilot project in about 25 rain gauge stations across 4 states in 2004. The products include insurance based on (a) seasonal rainfall; (b) sowing failure; (c) rainfall distribution; (d) agro-economic optimum index, and; (e) catastrophe cover. A private insurer has launched rainfall insurance in Mehabubnagar district of Andhra Pradesh. The insurance policy makes payments if the cumulative rainfall during the seasons is less than the historical average by more than predetermined threshold value. This is implemented on the basis of a rainfall index computed from rainfall during different periods, with weights based on the relative importance of rainfall during different periods.

It is important to recognise that in the long-term, risk preventive measures are likely to be more cost-effective. These include better water supplies in water stress periods, reducing ground water stress by grounding well-designed ground water recharge programmes through dug-well recharge, tank recharge and strengthening of water harvesting structures, instituting drought management system based on remote sensing methods, and household income diversification. Such preventive measures would reduce risk and thereby the premium rates of crop and weather insurance. But these would require a project approach to farm lending as most of the investments relating to ground water are in the private domain. No state has passed legislation preventing indiscriminate digging of wells. Spacing norms between dug-wells is a contentious issue and no state government would like to take any risk with the farmers' vote bank on this issue.

It is also necessary to strengthen crop surveillance mechanism for forecasting drought well in advance. This would facilitate the design and preparation of action plan for mitigating the adverse effect of drought on the farming community. The efforts of National Remote Sensing Agency (NRSA) based on satellite data at the district level for 10 drought-prone districts and at *mandal/taluka* level for 3 states, namely, Andhra Pradesh, Karnataka and Maharashtra, needs scaling up and wider dissemination for the preparation of action plans in the farm sector at the beginning of both kharif and rabi seasons. The crop assessment made at the end of the season could be utilised in crop insurance schemes.

Technology Risk Mitigation

Technology risk arises with the adoption of new crop cultural practices, new strains, and farm mechanization of a different order (related to a particular crop and not just tractorization). ICRISAT has contributed to introducing innovative instruments—mechanical threshers, low-cost weeders, etc. Government of India has introduced technology missions in crop specific areas like the Oil Technology Mission, Cotton Technology Mission (divided into four mini missions targeting production technology, extension, industry applications and marketing), and strategically moved in respect of certain crops like paddy in the eastern states, maize, etc. Certain area specific technology interventions through wasteland development and dry land tracts are in place.

Credit Risk Mitigation

Credit Risk starts from the origination itself. This origination level is targeted for mitigation through business correspondent/agent model and through banks' internal training systems. While the moral hazard is doubtful for avoidance, adverse selection could be easily avoided. In any case, a farmer is bound to be a more dependable borrower than other categories because of the fact that farmer and farm are inseparable from his livelihood perspective. All individual farm loans of under Rs 2 lakh are targeted for credit scoring by quite a few commercial banks. They take into consideration risks attendant on origination and transaction. At the origination level, they look to the age of the borrower, family size, present net agricultural income, type and extent of land holding and the crops traditionally in cultivation vis-à-vis the new ones, if any, being introduced, etc, and at the transaction level, crops grown, tangible/intangible security, collateral deposits, mortgage cover, conduct of the account, etc. In most parts of the country, banks have introduced KCC to assure credit for crop cultivation and other investments related to land, but their performance left much to be desired. The allegation is that this instrument contributed to banks showing the required number of accounts to the government.

Market Risk Mitigation

Prices and Markets

According to the Report of the Expert Committee on Agricultural Indebtedness (2007) set up by the PMO, "since price volatility is more pronounced in the world market, the integration of domestic agriculture with global trade, without putting in place necessary institutional arrangements such as monitoring of price and production trends in the world market, enhancing internal capacity to anticipate price changes in the world market, and developing required skills to manage variable tariff rate instrument to protect the domestic market, is likely to increase price volatility in the domestic market. Trade liberalization affected the domestic market prices of several agricultural commodities in the recent period, particularly those of plantation crops such as coffee, tea, rubber, pepper and dry land crops such as oil seeds. The small peasants growing plantation crops and oil seeds were hurt the most. The variable tariff rate instrument must be utilised for moderating the adverse impact of price fluctuations in the world market on domestic prices of agricultural commodities. Capability to operate the instrument should be developed. Efforts should be made to enhance the total factor productivity of agriculture to improve its competitiveness."

Market risk arises from (a) lack of access to market; (b) inadequate volumes acceptable to the market; (c) absence of post-harvest technologies, which in turn, contribute to disruptions in the value-chain and; (d) producing what the farmer knows and not what the market wants again because of information asymmetry and lack of confidence in the outcomes. Government of India's efforts in formulating model legislation—Agricultural Produce Marketing Act (Model Bill)—to bring about reforms in agricultural marketing did not meet with success, as this subject is in the concurrent legislation domain. The greedy *kutcha arthiyars* still rule the agricultural market yards. The farmer delivers the produce, waits for the payment, sometimes even at the uneconomic price. He has to make a few rounds to the *arthiyar* for realizing the value for the produce. The transaction cost is pushed up as a consequence, and also makes him a bad borrower to the financing bank. In respect of certain cereal crops, minimum support is available from the government. Here also, the delivery mechanisms leave a lot to be desired. The MSP is more on political than economic considerations in respect of paddy and wheat crops, as barely 5 to 6 states contribute to the food security system managed by the government through the Food Corporation of India and State Civil Supplies Corporations. In respect of paddy, since the procurement is mostly rice, a value-added product, it is mostly millers that get into the price advantage and not the farmer. Then there is contract farming. In this case, the contractor sensitizes the farmer to modern cultural practices, post-harvest methods leading to assured quality, packing and customer preferences.

Basel II guidelines of the RBI on credit risk indicate certain general disclosures for all banks. These are broadly divided into qualitative and quantitative disclosures. The qualitative aspects demand clear-cut definitions of past dues, and impaired (for accounting purposes) accounts, and the bank's credit risk management policy. Banks go by the definition of past dues given by the RBI itself. In the case of farm loans, past dues are defined as those remaining due beyond two crop seasons. Among the quantitative disclosures, they have to specify the total exposure; activity-based exposure; residual contractual maturity breakdown of assets and the amount of gross NPAs; net NPAs; movement of NPAs; and movement of provisions.

We have seen in the credit risk management of this sector, most crop loans and all loans backed by the collateral security of farm lands virtually amount to clean loans, notwithstanding the unencumbered title to the land to the holder and eventually the transfer, either as charge or mortgage (Section 6 of SARFAESI Act prohibits sale of land by the mortgagee in the event of mortgagor's default on the loan). The Basel II guidelines under comprehensive approach clearly specify: "Banks must have clear and robust procedures for the timely liquidation of collateral to ensure that any legal conditions required for declaring the default of the counterparty and liquidating the collateral are observed, and that collateral can be liquidated promptly." Thus even under the most favourable circumstances, credit risk for agriculture is going to weigh high on the capital provisioning. It is learnt that the RBI is mulling over providing a guarantee cover for all farm advances on the basis of the recommendations of an Internal Expert Committee that examined the issues of disaster management and farmers' suicides. There will be a host of issues associated with such a fund: the size of the fund, contributors to the fund, replenishment, claim procedures, management of the fund, etc. If this is treated on par with the sovereign guarantee, there will truly be reprieve for the banks in terms of capital to risk weighted assets under this segment.

Multiple Lines of Credit

There is no better way for a bank to ward off NPAs than to extend multiple lines of credit to small and marginal farmers, who constitute nearly 70 percent of the total farmers occupying 23 percent of the land holdings and whose demand for credit from institutional sources is aggressive, because most of them pursue crop farming, storage of the produce, dairy, backyard poultry/ fish pond cultivation and sheep/ goat rearing, and quite a few women of those households pursue non-farm activities either as members of SHGs or individually. It is not one loan repaying another but that the asset-yield of one loan would mitigate the risk of loss arising from another asset in the event of an adverse situation arising in the farmer's household. Each of these activities mentioned above is potentially viable and interdependent. Products from off-farm activities supplement the income of the household. The animal and bird waste is used organic manure. In times of natural calamity, unless all assets are extinguished at the same time, the loss of crop asset has potential in-built compensations in off-farm and non-farm activities. Ceteris paribus, one economic activity reinforces the other activity, and therefore, providing multiple lines of activities would itself act as insurance against the losses incurred in one or a few of them. However, this would require a careful loan origination process, which would be worth its while for a lending institution since it would reduce transaction cost for the farmer on the one hand and enhances interest income for the lending institution. The instrument could be a SMART card for the farmer with a comprehensive credit limit with biometric application.

In conclusion, the burden of this article rests on the criticality of the Basel II interpretations and facilitation provided by the regulator. While some banks are seeing structuring loans on corporate lines, and some others linking up with microfinance entities like the SHGs, the broad question remains whether the farmer could be given different loan products and multiple loans with ability to cross-holding of risks. Presently what he gets, if at all, is a term loan, and mostly, a loan for working capital in the shape of crop finance that is mostly a mathematical exercise based on the scale of finance for each crop decided by the NABARD (the apex bank to look after the sector), multiplied by the number of hectares cultivated under each crop. The two basic risks—one, related to the farmer, and the other related to the farming activity—need to be addressed in terms of adverse selection, moral hazard and information asymmetry.

Notes

1. Sidharth Sinha, 2004, "Agricultural Insurance In India: Scope for Participation of Private Insurance," *Economic and Political Weekly*, 39(25).
2. G.S. Bhalla, 2007, *Indian Agriculture Since Independence*, National Book Trust.

References

Shovan Ray, 2007, *Hand Book of Agriculture*, New Delhi: Oxford University Press.

B. Yerram Raju, 2006-07, Annual Report, RBI, Mumbai.

Raju, 2007, "Expert Committee on Agricultural Indebtedness", Mumbai: NABARD.

CHAPTER 17

Governance in Agriculture

M.S. Swaminathan, recalling the combat with the Bengal famine, observes rightly: "If agriculture goes wrong, nothing else will have a chance to go right in this country".[1] Except the unleashing of a National Policy for Farmers in 2007[2], that still is crying for implementation, nothing seems to have gone right in the agricultural sector. Farmers' suicides continue still in agriculture-intensive states like Andhra Pradesh, Karnataka, Punjab, etc. There are regions where farmers declared a crop holiday to demonstrate their anger against poor governance. The purpose of this article is to address the issue of governance in this sector.

Ministries Influencing the Farm Sector

No other sector in the country besides agriculture is in the stranglehold of a number of inter-connected Ministries at the centre: Union Ministries of Agriculture and Cooperation; Water Resources; Food Processing Industries; Rural Development; Commerce (dealing with international trade) and Industry; Environment and Forests; Micro, Small and Medium Enterprises; Consumer Affairs and Public Distribution, Science and Technology; Non-Conventional Energy Sources; Finance and above all; the Planning Commission. Agriculture being a concurrent subject in the Constitution of India, the states have as many corresponding Ministries that interact with the central government in governing this farm sector. I have not come across another country that governs the farm sector through such a web of governance. Each Ministry and each state government has its own last word that rarely matches with the other. Finally the farmer stands at a disadvantage finally.

It is politically infeasible to reduce the number of Ministries, either at the state or centre, for the simple reason that each stratum of the fragmented democracy should get a berth in the seat of power. But after 6.5 decades of independence, having successfully combated the famine, having moved to impressive ranks in the world with milk, poultry, horticulture, etc, in production, we are far away from providing food security. Forty percent of production is still wasted or rotting in the government warehouses, a situation that even invited the wrath of the Supreme Court to correct the situation with expedition.

The Cabinet Sub-Committees at the centre and states that constitute a coordinated mechanism for releasing the policies related to agriculture, or for that matter, any other policy, are the only coordination forums now functioning. The oversight mechanism for monitoring and concurrent evaluation of the functioning of regulatory institutions suffers from lack of such coordination. There is no regulatory impact assessment of any policy and regulation as an ongoing exercise like in the UK.

We are living in a fast-changing and dynamic world requiring quick and correct responses. Land and water resources, the principal factors of production in the farm sector, are scarce but the bourgeoning population adds pressure year after year on these scarce resources. Resources like water, soil, plants and animal life have the capacity to regenerate but the speed may not cope with the ever-increasing demand on them. Sub-division and fragmentation of holdings, riparian water resources and shrinking farm labour, coupled with rising consumer expectations for quality food and water, make the governance complex. If the farmer has one cow in his backyard, it will take care of his organic manure requirements of one acre of cultivable land. But the cow is with animal husbandry department; backyard is with panchayati raj department, manure is with department of agriculture and bio-diversity; and land is with the revenue department. This is where governance matters as each department moves to regulate its own area according to what it thinks, right and not what is right.

What do we mean by 'Governance'?

Wikipedia defines: "Governance is the act of governing. It relates to decisions that define *expectations,* grant power, or verify performance. It consists of either a separate process or part of decision-making or leadership processes." Governance relates to consistent management, cohesive policies, guidance, processes and decision-rights for a given area of responsibility. This stands on the four pillars of decentralization, accountability, transparency, and coordination. It embraces action by executive bodies, legislatures and Parliament and judicial bodies (from the local levels to the Supreme Court, the highest judiciary).

In the post-liberalization era, governance has been the most discussed subject but is like the four blind men trying to define an elephant. It has resulted in assertion and acceptance of certain rights for good: the right to work; the right to information; and the right to safety and security for every citizen. Some have already taken the effect of legal sanctity and are yet trying to find space for functional existence. Since my focus is on governance in the farm sector, I would try to look at areas that need reform viewing from the interest of the farmer, the centre of attention.

The reform in governance, in so far as the farm sector is concerned, should start from understanding the complexity of the farming, the farmer and his family and the society in which he lives, and to which he contributes most. Philosophically speaking, if I receive something, I should be in a position to return something to the giver. The farmer gives me food and makes me live, and therefore, the least I can give him is to provide conditions that continue to enable him to live happily and continue to give me all that I want to feed myself, my family and my dependents.

How does this happen in the diverse and complex area of governance that we have today? Implementation of multiple schemes and programmes by different departments and Ministries for the farmer has led to centralization.

Decentralization of administration, the first principle of governance, in the absence of the focused attention on the target led to misdistribution of scarce resources and the equity has become a casualty in the name of equality. Conceptual correction is required at the point of decentralization. How is the decentralization process involving the farmer at the lowest level of administration—the panchayat?

Accountability is the next principle, demanding performance not just from the point of view of a financial goal but from the point of view of how this target of governance has improved—the lot of the small farmer, the marginal farmer, the landless labourer, and the tenant, in the overall framework of farming.

Transparency is the third principle of governance. How is this achieved? Has information technology been effectively used in communicating to the farmer all that he needs to produce, store and market, and earn a cost plus to continue in production with dignity and honour? Mobile technology has made rapid strides in passing on information from the learned to the learning, and also for effecting payments and receipts. How much investment is required to take this technology within the operating convenience of the illiterate and semi-literate soiled palm of the farmer? Responses to these questions have the potential to resolve the information asymmetry of the farmer in remunerative technology adoption.

Coordination is the fourth principle of governance, the real villain of the piece. How can this be achieved?

In all the states—that is, nearly about twelve that have preponderance of agriculture as the driving force of their growth and are also carrying the burden of growth of the rest of the economy and at the centre, an agricultural vision document should be prepared after a thorough inquest by the agriculture, animal husbandry and horticulture universities in the state, as a first step. This vision document should be shared with all the stakeholders and the scientists within a set timeframe. This document shall lay down the objectives and goals of farm policy and coordination mechanism.

Second, each of those states shall prepare annual agricultural sectors surveys with the farming related universities in the lead, and this annual survey should be presented before the Legislative Assembly, a day ahead of the presentation of the Agriculture Budget that should also be presented every year ahead of the General Budget session. This Budget shall be subsumed in the General Budget. This process would make sure that the finances of the state move in tandem with the requirements of the farmers.[3]

Third, once in 2 months, the Coordinating Forum on Agriculture (COFA) with the Minister of Agriculture (could be designated as Deputy Chief Minister in such states) presiding, should review the budget releases and ensure that the lowest level of delivery gets the physical resources to be in the reach of the farmers. This COFA shall be vested with the authority of vetoing any proposals and censuring any actions of those that run counter the effective implementation of the policy goals in agriculture.

Networking is the name of good governance. Technology should help take innovations and research on the field to the lab for commercial assessment, and the Indian Council of Agricultural Research and the farm extension wings in the states should spearhead this area and for backward integration.

Agriculture marketing needs to move from the politicians to the farmers. This would require change in the Agriculture Marketing Acts of the states and huge investments in technology at each market yard where the farmer is comfortable with unloading his produce, with the swiping of his SMART card, and walks away with cash into his bank account. Improving governance in this area holds the key as, in all the other areas, we have reached some milestones that can be moved forward faster than a few decades ago. Let us resolve to make agriculture right to make sure that everything else in the country goes right.

Notes

1. M.S. Swaminathan, 2013, "From Bengal Famine to Right to Food", *The Hindu*, 13 February.
2. Swaminathan, 2008, "Agricultural Strategy, Internal Security and Sovereignty", *The Hindu*, 1 January.

Reference

B. Yerram Raju, 2013, *Inclusion Journal*, January–March.

CHAPTER 18

The Way Forward

Agriculture has been blamed more on the weather gods than on the vagaries of many a bureaucrat and on those who committed wanton acts of neglect in implementing even right policies. Politicians should take as much should of the blame as the rest.

Some great savants like late C. Subrahmanyam, who was Union Minister for Agriculture, spread out the red carpet for the farmers and late Prime Minister Lal Bahadur Shastri, who raised the slogan *Jai Jawan, Jai Kisan* and provided direction to the country's development agenda. There are eminent scientists like M.S. Swaminathan, who did the country proud through several scientific innovations in agriculture, and also provided a direction to the Agriculture Policy of the country. There are journalists like P. Sainath of *The Hindu,* who with several incisive stories, exposed the ills faced by the farmers and farm labour.

After years of neglect at the macro level, marked by inadequate capital formation in the agricultural sector, the policies of the 1990s were directed to compressing the staff and other government expenditure. When the production-oriented sector suffers inadequacies continuously for a decade or so, particularly, in the area of HR, it only leads to devastating results. Structural deficiencies continue. Small farmers have become marginal farmers and marginal farmers have become agricultural labourers. In fact, with wages rising in the farm sector, marginal farmers have found it more advantageous to drift to farm labour than the small farmers, as reinforced by our own field study analysis. Imbalances in labour markets caused by MGNREGA triggered efforts for mechanization of farming and technology is proving its edge in cost-benefit ratios. The resources required—physical, technical, financial and human—both in terms of effort and spread, demand huge outlays year after year. There is, therefore, no room for complacence.

Although famines became a thing of the past because of farmers quickly adopting innovations and technology, drought and suicides of farmers remain a continuing phenomena. Shortage and wastage have become synonymous with agriculture. Misdirected agenda of the government and faulty land use policies have often become points of debate of both the state legislatures and Parliament. While taking a long journey into the historical expression of many such issues, I have suggested, at several points of time, corrective measures that can still be considered valid, and this book can have a take-away for the readers and policy makers in this chapter.

Governance

In the agriculture dominant states, Agriculture Budget should be presented ahead of the General Budget of the state preceded by a survey of agriculture to be done by the state agriculture universities with one of the Vice Chancellors spearheading the team.

It is highly desirable to prune the number of Ministries revolving round the farmer. If it is not politically expedient to do so, there must be a coordinated mechanism at the central, state and sub-state levels–COFA chaired by the Minister for Agriculture. COFA would review quarterly budget allocations and expenditures to ensure that the seasons do not miss out in the allocations, and expenditure earmarked for all the sub-sectors move in tandem. COFA should have authority to summon the errand and also to ensure corrective action in time.

Both these measures would ensure transparency, accountability and responsibility for responding to the farmers' requirements in good time.

Research and Extension

These are the 2 eyes of agriculture development. Technology is already making inroads in ensuring that the farmer would have access to the scientist in resolving the field level problems at least cost, through mobile communications. Wider and widespread applications throughout the country in all regional languages should be quickly organized. Further, proper and timely dissemination of best practices should be given the attention of the universities and ICAR institutions.

Experiences in states like Andhra Pradesh and Karnataka suggest that the government should support formation of farmers' societies (not necessarily cooperative) on the lines of vegetables farmers' societies in Bangalore, who engage on a regular basis, cold storage vans to sell vegetables in up-end and high-margin earning metro markets.

Agri-Tourism also has good prospects that would earn revenues both to the government and the farmers.

Regulation

1. There are also issues of regulation. Many farmers, with a view to come out of the debt trap, anxiously jumped into cotton cultivation despite being aware of the high risks. They get into a vicious circle. Such situations can be corrected through regulatory mechanism. Similarities can be drawn from the type of interventions Andhra Pradesh made with respect to tobacco. It is also important that indiscriminate digging of borewells is regulated through legislation so that the mere availability of a bore does not enthuse a farmer to take to irrigated or irrigated dry crops. Deep borewells are proving inefficient, both from the point of view of irrigation and power. They consume energy far more than the yield generated.
2. Agriculture Department currently is performing both facilitating (credit, fertilizers, natural resource improvement) and regulating functions (seeds, pesticides, etc.). In view of the need for greater role in extension and facilitation of the department, it is desirable to separate out the functions of regulation as the conflict of interest in protecting the interests of farmers versus other groups can be overcome only through such measures.

Agriculture Credit

Targets for subsidized credit have taken a toll on the agricultural credit portfolio. The targets have a slant for crop loans during the last 10 years. The result was that private capital formation in agriculture has taken a backseat investment credit in agriculture has not moved up from 1990–91. While there is a broad realization that the Multi-Agency Approach to agricultural credit is here to stay, lopsided attention to rural cooperative credit system and unsupervised credit from the other agencies rendered the credit for farm sector ineffective. All the projects in the farm sector should target an increase in farm income as the raison d'être of farm investment.

The basis for arriving at the 18 percent aggregate credit for agriculture requires modification.

Allocations for small and marginal farmers should have specific monitorable targets both under investment and short-term credit.

The government should encourage mixed farming, particularly for small, marginal, and sub-marginal farmers, so that one productive activity will counter the distress arising from other losing farming activity. Bank credit, if given for such multiple activities, would itself ensure speedy repayments as market vulnerabilities are reduced.

In the context of declining position of capital formation in agriculture, the banks should campaign aggressively for provision of medium- and long-term capital loans for agriculture and allied sectors by adopting appropriate strategies. The role of NABARD need not be over emphasized in this regard.

Allocations for dry land cultivation, waste land development, and watershed management at the sub-state level should be scientifically arrived at and monitored regularly by the State Level Coordination Committee of bankers. COFA should invite the President, SLBC or Regional Head of NABARD to submit the review report at its quarterly committee meetings.

Sharecroppers and tenants have not received the attention they deserved from the credit agencies because of appropriate insurance mechanisms. The initiative of Government of Andhra Pradesh is faulty in law and ineffective in implementation. The Joint Liability Group lending has also not picked up. A bankers' committee with the NABARD Chairman at the helm should be set up to examine the issues involved and evolve appropriate policies for implementation so that the producers' and lenders' interests are adequately taken care of. Accepted recommendations should be mandated for implementation with appropriate penal provisions for non-implementation.

Investments in critical areas like biotechnology and information technology should have specific allocations from both government and credit institutions and these should have specific timelines for implementation with regional professional committees for monitoring and implementation.

The recommendations of the M.V. Nair Committee are lopsided and need correction to serve the interests of the farmers and not the farm overlords. Prioritization has taken a queer turn with such recommendations. Corrections do not brook delay.

Unsupervised and armchair lending for agriculture is the villain of the piece. All the financing institutions should be enjoined upon to supervise agriculture credit and also to ensure that banks devote enough time and attention for extension as the key to making credit effective.

1. Provision of minor irrigation facilities (in non-dark areas) including renovation of tanks wherever possible with a huge subsidy component.
2. Provision of subsidized quality inputs (seed and fertilizers/pesticides) to SFs/MFs. The government should ensure that spurious and adulterated inputs do not go out of their own vaults. The mechanism for settling cases relating to damage on account of spurious seeds should be speeded up, and claims should be settled within a fortnight.
3. While the free power tariff provided a great relief to the farming community, there is an imperative need on the part of the government to strictly ensure uninterrupted quality supply of power for the required number of hours, by maintaining appropriate standards for service lines.
4. Interest rate on agricultural loans to SFs and MFs (including tenant farmers up to the same land ceiling) should be at 3 percent lesser than that of the interest on loans to other farmers.
5. The scheme of distribution of farm implements/ machinery should be expanded so as to cover all the SFs/MFs in 2 or 3 years.
6. Provision of loans to other allied and non-farm activities (e.g. dairy, sheep rearing, fish rearing, etc) alongside agriculture to the farmers as a basket of combined activities.
7. Weaning away the farmers from private moneylenders by appropriate credit counselling and rigorous application of related laws against the moneylenders.

KCC has, to a large extent, modified and should be linked to the ATMs and merchandise for purchase of inputs. The Card should have details of the farmer, his holding size and nature, irrigation facilities, and the number of dependent family members so that swiping the card would enable the banker to assess the suitability of the crops and credit requirements.

Marketing holds the key to success for the farmer and the credit agency. Wherever and whenever the farmers fail to secure the cost of production plus reasonable profit as take-home benefit from his long toil in the till, the state should have mechanism to supplement the shortfall.

Providing adequate market support to farmers through market intervention and offering realistic price for different crops.

Insurance

Insurance mechanisms also require re-orientation to the needs of the farmer. Natural calamities require specific efforts of bail-out packages. Droughts, cyclones, floods, holocausts, hurricanes and tsunamis have different impacts on the field. The treatment and dispensation of relief packages shall undergo a revamp.

1. Free crop insurance to SFs/MFs and 50 percent subsidy in premium for other farmers (for the next 3 years).
2. Crop insurance scheme should be modified so as to make it more farmer-centric and crop-oriented instead of loan-related and area-oriented.

Last, but not the least, NABARD should rethink and re-orient its structure to suit its original mandate to help agriculture and rural development. 3 decades down the line, its performance does not speak well when it comes to the supervisory role it performed over the RRBs and cooperative credit institutions, whose share in farm credit has come down drastically during this period.

Sustainable agricultural growth of 4 percent and over during the next 10 years is imperative for the economy to attain an accelerated growth of 9 percent and above. "If agriculture fails, nothing else can hope to succeed in this country."

Post Script

Food Security Act 2013 and its Implications on the Future

At the time when this book is about to be published, Lok Sabha passed the Food Security Act 2013 on 27 August, 2013. I thought it would be appropriate to put this post script at the suggestion of the publisher's editor.

The Act made its way in an otherwise turbulent political environment where the government has been facing the House with explanations on various scandals; the fall of the rupee with the resultant deterioration in the current account deficit and on top of it, the fiscal deficit set to reach an unsustainable level, if the Food Security Act were to get implemented. All the parties supported the bill as none would like to be dubbed as anti-poor with the impending General Elections. The purpose of this chapter is to discuss the pros and cons of the various provisions of the Act in terms of its implementation.

World Food Summit (13–17 November, 1996) defined Food Security as: "Food security exists when all people, at all times, have physical and economic access to sufficient, safe and nutritious food to meet their dietary needs and food preferences for an active and healthy life." Although India could distance famines, it could not stall starvation deaths. Its lead in paddy and wheat production would seem to be at the cost of production in millets and other course cereals and pulses and oil seeds. Both calories and proteins remained below the recommended dietary levels. The country acquired the dubious distinction of housing 300mn poor, by whatever definition one defines the poor. There has been a multiplicity of schemes that targeted such poor only to ensure that they remain at that level for granting political largesse through bureaucratic extravaganza. This contextual frame helps one to look at the Food Security Act 2013 of Government of India that provided staple food grains to all the Below Poverty Line (BPL) families uniformly across the country. There has been a drubbing by the Supreme Court over the mounting food stocks in the Food Corporation of India (FCI) warehouses and people reporting starvation deaths in one or the other part of the country that speeded up the legislative process.

The Right to Food as a fundamental right cannot be ensured by a series of intentions. In a country of diversities in both economic (size of the poorer sections of population and their identification differ across the states) and political spectrum, where the resources for taking care of the poor have to be provided by the states more than the centre, a Central Act like the Food Security Act is more a political gimmick than an economic tool. This Act, to quote K.R. Venugopal, "is like dropping a coin in the Bay of Bengal and searching for it in Indian Ocean." Several fundamental needs like water, sanitation and power are essential as much as mere food and without them the food security could turn out as insecure. Even after 66 years of independence, we have more than 40 percent of villages not having access to safe drinking water and secured health.

It is unfortunate that the key observations of the Food and Agriculture Organization (FAO) in its paper on "The State of Food Insecurity in the World", 2011 have received only lip service:

> A food-security strategy that relies on a combination of increased productivity in agriculture, greater policy predictability and general openness to trade will be more effective than other strategies;
>
> Safety nets are crucial for alleviating food insecurity in the short term, as well as for providing a foundation for long-term development;
>
> High food prices present incentives for increased long-term investment in the agriculture sector, which can contribute to improved food security in the longer term[1].

Schedule II of the Act contains provisions relating to reforms to the agricultural sector that needed attention. Assuring sustained increase in production consistent with the growing requirements of the Act and the resources that the states should provide for implementing the Act are vital components of the agenda but receive scant attention. As the Commission for Agriculture Costs and Prices (CACP) points out "Assured procurement gives an incentive for farmers to produce cereals rather than diversify the production-basket…Vegetable production too may be affected—pushing food inflation further." If these cereals do not find attractive prices and specific support prices for those that are part of the food security system, there would be serious consequences for the farm economy.

Priority Category

Definition of the poor has come into serious controversy lately. The criteria have to be fully in public knowledge. While the Act specified that the records have to be transparent and in the public domain, there is no timeframe for doing so by the states. So is the case for another requirement under the Act: "that the states shall put in place the needed information, communication and technology systems in place."

The list of the eligible families should be displayed at the village panchayat level and at the ward level in the urban municipalities. Any divergence of opinion has to be resolved at the village/ local level within one week of placing the list on notice. Such list could be prepared through a survey done by NGOs or educational institutions at the block/*mandal* levels.

All those who are within the exempted income category for payment of income tax should become eligible for food entitlement under the food security provisions.

All the tax-payers shall be the excluded category for two reasons: they have the ability to buy the food because they have regular income; they are also otherwise covered by some social security provision or the other.

Nutrition security is the whole while food security is a part of that, and therefore the law that is being contemplated should really have been a food-cum-nutrition security law rather than a mere food security law.

It is also worth noting at the outset that an important strategy for defending and expanding the rights of the poor in any scheme that seeks to guarantee a particular right is to fine-tune it to the other related schemes in a manner that all related schemes pull together all the rights that govern all the participants in such schemes. Such a synergy will guarantee all rights essential to the poor, each right reinforcing the other. Food and nutrition security is no exception to such a synergy. In fact the most important paradigm that should govern a law that guarantees food-cum-nutrition security is to define such security as the total sum of the entitlement that a poor household would access through its entitlement in all the food and nutrition related schemes that the government implements or proposes to implement and not merely through a single programme like the Targeted Public Distribution System (TPDS). Unfortunately, the Act failed to provide this comprehensiveness.

The Food Security Act 2013 guarantees 5 kg of rice, wheat and coarse cereals per month per individual at a fixed price of Rs 3, 2, and 1, respectively, to nearly 75 percent of the rural and 50 percent of the urban population.

The government estimates suggest that food security will cost Rs 1,24,723 crore per year. But that is just one estimate. Andy Mukherjee, a columnist with Reuters, puts the cost at around $25 billion. The Commission for Agricultural Costs and Prices (CACP) of the Ministry of Agriculture in a research paper titled "National Food Security Bill: Challenges and Options" puts the cost of the food security scheme over a three-year period at Rs 6,82,163 crore. During the first year the cost to the government has been estimated at Rs 2,41,263 crore.

Economist Surjit Bhalla in a column in *The Indian Express* put the cost of the bill at Rs 3,14,000 crore or around 3 percent of the GDP. Ashok Kotwal, Milind Murugkar and Bharat Ramaswami challenge Bhalla's calculation in a column in *The Financial Express* and write, "the food subsidy bill should... come to around 1.35 percent of GDP, which is still way less than the numbers he (Bhalla) put out."

When we look at the Budgeted Receipts of the government for 2013–14, presuming that such receipts would come even at the declining growth expectations, they are just Rs 11,22,799 crore. The government's estimated cost of food security comes at 11.10 percent (Rs 1,24,723 expressed as a percentage of Rs 11,22,799 crore) of the total receipts. The CACP's estimated cost of food security comes at 21.5 percent (Rs 2,41,263 crore expressed as a percentage of Rs 11,22,799 crore) of the total receipts. Bhalla's cost of food security comes at around 28 percent of the total receipts (Rs 3,14,000 crore expressed as a percentage of Rs 11,22,799 crore). Where do you find the money to implement the schemes?

The CACP estimates an expenditure of Rs 6,82,183 crore in the first three years of launching the scheme, with Rs 2,41,263 crore in the first year itself. If the scheme is initiated in 2013–14, the gross fiscal deficit of the centre would substantially shoot-up to 6.7 percent of GDP, a level not reached since 1993–94[2]. The states' finances are moving at alarming debt rates.

Implementation is at the doorsteps of the state governments while the stocks are with the central government and the coordination between the two would require being nonpartisan and wholehearted.

This apart, the administrative expenses for setting up the State Food Commission, District Grievance Cells, and the Vigilance Teams and for the implementation of ICT across the state right up to the village level and integrating with the entire distribution system cutting across panchayats, cooperatives, private licensed traders, etc., have to be incurred by the state governments. CACP has also indicated that "additional expenses have to be incurred for scaling up of operations, enhancement of production, investments for storage, movement, processing and market infrastructure, etc." There is no ballpark figure in the approach papers.

As against the National Advisory Council (NAC) recommendation of 35 kg of food grains per month, the Act provides for only 25 kg in the Public Distribution System (PDS) in one-fourth of the most disadvantaged districts or blocks in the country in the first year given the fact that an average household of 5 would need the energy equivalent of around 60 kg of food grains per month. Therefore the law should have specifically referred to all the food and nutrition-related schemes as also schemes where the potential exists for the use of essential commodities (like in the MGNREGA) together and examine how much a poor household would access through all these programmes through organically integrating them at the delivery level. Complementarities of the existing programmes require recognition and integration.

It is important to add that all these programmes need to be predicated on adequate, decentralized production of food grains which essentially means that India's dry land agriculture must receive priority attention by way of a second green revolution in the vast areas of the country that do not have assured irrigation facilities. This emphasis is found missing in the Act.

It is essential to change the provision in the MGNREGA in regard to this basic issue from guaranteeing just 100 days of employment to the entire household to guaranteeing 100 days of employment to every adult in a household. While on this, a point has been made that the second most important objective of MGNREGA, provision of livelihood opportunities, has been almost a forgotten goal. It is important to realize that people should be earning while contributing to production and not just for attendance. The skewed nature of MGNREGA as voiced in the farm sector created serious imbalances in terms of availability of labour at the time when farmers require labour. Even the small and marginal farmers are now shifting to technology and such shift would also have long-term implications to soil fertility. The deeper the plough, the larger the deprivation of soil fertility. The vicious cycle of productivity sets in. This should be avoided through appropriate policy intervention.

The households living below the poverty line, identified through transparent and liberal criteria such as through surveys conducted at the grassroots level by agencies of decentralized governance, with assistance from civil society groups, need a properly targeted, functioning, and affordable PDS, in addition to a proper wage employment guarantee programme as described *supra,* to cope with their food security needs. To ensure this, the price of food grains in a well-run TPDS should be determined on the basis of the employment levels and wage levels obtained at the relevant time. The size of the family should be the unit to determine the food requirements of the household, ensuring interpersonal equity within the household concerning scales. Such requirement should be guaranteed to a poor household as its non-negotiable entitlement.

An average household needs to be supplied 720 kg of cereals per annum to ensure its cereals security (60 kg x 12). The bulk of it must come from the cereal wage component of the MGNREGA wage. At 200 days of employment the cereals that can be accessed will be 500 kg (200 x 2.5 kg). In such a scenario, the TPDS should provide the balance. The law should have therefore calibrated what the cereals policy should be in the MGNREGA's wage composition first before determining what it should be in the TPDS, for the vast unorganized labour that participates in the MGNREGA. If the MGNREGA would not provide for an optimum number of days of guaranteed employment or the cereal wage component, then the burden of cereals security would fall entirely on the TPDS to the extent of supplying 60 kg per household per month on an average or to the extent of non-provision of employment. Sixty kg is mentioned as an average because household sizes would obviously differ but the overall national need will have to be calculated on the basis of the total poor households to be guaranteed food at this scale. Such planning for all poor households is essential since not all the poor would be participating in the MGNREGA.

It need hardly be added that cereals alone do not mean food. To begin with, at least, pulses, edible oil and iodised salt need to be added to this basket, with emphasis on the supply of nutritious cereals like jowar, ragi, bajra and other "minor" millets. The quantity of entitlement and the affordable price fixed should be kept frozen for the period during which the household remains below the poverty line, the elimination of such poverty itself being the acid test of the quality and implementation of the development and anti-poverty strategies drawn up by the state.

Antyodaya Anna Yojana scheme being implemented through Anganwadis and the mid-day meal programme have been rightly clubbed with the provisions of the Act but the mechanisms are totally ill-equipped and we have in the recent past instances in Bihar, and elsewhere, seen the disasters of several children getting killed after swallowing the mid-day meal in the school.

The TPDS should thus be looked upon as an alternate market for the poor, but it can function as a market relevant to the poor only when insulated from factors of violent fluctuations of supplies and price. It is also desirable to dispense the ration shops and introduce food coupons with the entitlements clearly indicated so that the poor can draw their entitlement when they have income in their hands and at any time during the day. There is merit in this argument for building into the new law. While the Act does provide for cash transfers, food coupons and other schemes, this would appear as an administrative protectionist window.

The Scheme is open-ended and has no specific directions to target the needy. It also does not have any specific deadlines for setting up various institutions mentioned in the Act like the District Grievance Cells, State Food Commission, Vigilance Committees and the setting up of ICT to cope with the tasks outlined in the Act for the related departments.

The saving grace of the Act has been that the responsibility for "creating, maintaining, modern and scientific storage facilities at various levels shall vest with central government." The open warehouses under the tarpaulins and the poorly maintained FCI warehouses amply demonstrate the inadequacies of the concerned departments to address this responsibility different from those that exist currently.

This Act can have the dubious distinction of fixing no accountability for failure to implement any of the provisions of the Act excepting to state that malaises in implementation would be dealt with as per the criminal procedure code. We are aware as to how long would such proceedings take and the impunity with which the errand can move about until the cases are settled. The Act makes good politics and bad economics in one stroke. Who can love the poor more than the politicians of India for in them rests the vote bank still? Everybody wants food security but along with it think of providing safe drinking water as a couple of glasses of safe drinking water are as important as nutritious food. The lactating mothers need it all the more. This should join the mission mode for ensuring food security.

Notes

1. IFAD, WFP and FAO, 2011.
2. Charan Singh, 2013, "Food Security Bill, Where is the Money?" *The Hindu Business Line*, 7 August.

References

K.R. Venugopal, 2010, "On the NAC's Innocence of Food Security Issue", *Economic Political Weekly*, 27 November.

Venugopal, 2010, "The National Food Security Act, 2010", *Social Change Journal*, Council for Social Development, December.

B. Yerram Raju, 2011, Round Table on the Draft Food Security Bill September 2011, PSA, 9 October.

Select Bibliography

Abbott, John C., 1987, *Agricultural Marketing Enterprises for the Developing World*, Cambridge University Press.

Acharya S.S., "Agricultural Marketing: Issues and Challenges", *Indian Journal of Agricultural Economics*, Vol. 53(3), pp. 98 and 311–13.

Bhalla, G.S., 2007, *Indian Agriculture Since Independence*, National Book Trust.

Clayton, Eric, 1975, *Agricultural Employment Creation and Small Holder, Rubber Production in Sumatra: Issue 2 of Occasional Paper*, Wye College, Agrarian development Unit.

———, 1983, *Agriculture, Poverty & Freedom in Developing Countries*, Macmillan Publications, pp. 185 and 187.

Gittinger, J. Price, *Economic Analysis of Agricultural Projects*, Bombay, A World Bank Publications, reprinted by ARDC, p. 1.

Harriss–White, Barbara, 1996, *A Political Economy of Agricultural Markets in South India*, pp. 307–337, 341.

Kundu, A., 2004, "Country Study on Right to Food", India: Food and Agriculture Organization.

Nadri, K., Schmitz, H., 1994, "Industrial clusters in less Developed Countries: Review of Experiences and Research Agenda", Discussion Paper 339, Institute of Development Studies, University of Sussex.

Prasad, Jagadish and Arabind Prasad, 1995, (ed.), *Indian Agricultural marketing, Emerging Trends and Perspectives*, Mittall Publications.

Ray, Shovan, 2007, *Hand Book of Agriculture*, New Delhi: Oxford University Press.

Singh, Charan, 2013, "Food Security Bill, Where is the Money?", *The Hindu Business Line*, 7, August.

Sinha, Sidharth, 2004, "Agricultural Insurance In India: Scope for Participation of Private Insurance", *Economic and Political Weekly*, 39(25).

Swaminathan, M.S., 2008, "Agricultural Strategy, Internal Security and Sovereignty", *The Hindu*, 1 January.

———, 2013, "From Bengal Famine to Right to Food", *The Hindu*, 13 February.

Talwar, R.K, 1970, "Expert Group on State Enactments", Ch.7, p. 31.

Venugopal, K.R., 2010, "On the NAC's Innocence of Food Security Issue", *Economic Political Weekly*, 27 November.

———, 2010, "The National Food Security Act, 2010", *Social Change Journal*, Council for Social Development, December.

Wilson, Kalpana, 2002, "Small Cultivators in Bihar and 'New' Technology", *Economic and Political Weekly*, 37(13).

Yerram Raju, B, 1954, All India Rural Credit Survey Committee, RBI.

———, 1969, AIRCS Report.

———, 1978, Kamath Committee Report, RBI.

———, 1978, Working Group on Regional Rural Banks, RBI.

———, 1981, "The Tasks before the National Bank for Agriculture and Rural Development", *The Hindu*, 29 December.

———, 1982, Committee to Review Arrangements for Agriculture and Rural Development, RBI.

———, 1985, "Disaster Management: Role of Financial Institutions", *Economic Times*, 25 January.

———, 1985, "Rural Banking: A perspective for Rural Development", *Financing Agriculture: January–March*.

———, 1987, ACRC.

———, 1987, Agricultural Credit Review Committee, RBI, pp. 881–923.

———, 1987, "Impact of Technology on Indian Agriculture", Impact of Technology on Development, Andhra University, 22 March, Visakhapatnam.

———, 1988, "Institutional Credit and Role of Voluntary Agencies in Rural Development", *Journal of Rural Development*, 7(6), Hyderabad, National Institute of Rural Development, pp. 723–728.

———, 1988, "Rural Credit: Issues in Planning and Policy", *IBA Bulletin: December*, Mumbai, pp. 275–276.

———, 1991, "The Need for and Imperatives of a Rural Credit Policy", *The Financial Express*.

———, 1991, "Social Banking and Profitability", *Agriculture Credit Policy and Small Farmer Bias: An Analysis*, (ed.) C.R. Kothari, Jaipur: Arihant Publishers, Chapter 12.

———, 1992, "Project Sustainability in Indian Agriculture", *Prashasan Journal*, Rajasthan Institute of Public Administration.

——— and Yugandhar, B.N., 1992, "Government Delivery Systems for Rural Development: Malady-Remedy Analysis", *Economic & Political Weekly*, 27(35), Mumbai.

———, 1993, "A strategy for sustainable projects for the poor", *NABARD Newsletter* 4(5), 1 August, Mumbai.

———, 1993–94, NSS 50th Round.

———, 1994, "Directed Credit Programmes— Which way to go?", *SBI Monthly Review: January*, Mumbai.

———, 1994, *Project Finance for Agriculture*, Jaipur: Prashasan.

———, 1997, "Agricultural Credit by Commercial Banks in India: Analytical framework for Reform", *Liberalization and the Small Farmer*, Y.V. Krishna Rao (ed.) AIKS, Hyderabad: ILO publication, Chapter 6, pp. 68–87.

———, 1997–98, Currency and Finance, Mumbai, RBI, Vol. I, Vols 13 to 45.

———, 1997, Gupta Committee, RBI.

———, 1998, "Giving Due Credit to the Farm Sector", *IBA Bulletin: November*, Mumbai.

———, 1998, PROBITY, Mumbai, October, Ch.3 pp. 3–1 to 3–2.

———, 1999, "Financing Farmers for Agricultural Marketing", *IBA Bulletin: November*, Mumbai.

———, 2001, "Challenge to farm sector", *The Hindu Business Line*, 18 September.

———, 2001, "Farm Credit: Banks must be more proactive", *The Hindu Business Line*, 31 July.

———, 2002, "Land Information System", *The Hindu Business Line*, 16 August.

———, Rao, N.G.P., 2001, (ed.), *Andhra Pradesh Vision 2020: Strategy for Sustainable Agricultural Growth*, New Delhi: New Age International Publishers.

———, Varkki, S, 2002, "WTO and Indian Agriculture: Challenges and Responsibilities", Paper presented for the National Seminar on WTO, organized by the Indian Institute of Foreign Trade, New Delhi, 2-3 February.

———, 2002, World Development Report, p. 39.

———, 2002, World Development Report, p. 45.

———, 2003, Cooperatives as Sustainable Means for Agricultural Production and Marketing: Text of the paper presented at The 56th All India Commerce Conference at Jalgaon, 25–26 December.

———, 2003, "Searching for Small and Marginal Farmers", *The Financial Express*, 10, March.

———, 2004, "Building Competitiveness in Rice", *Commodity Review: November*, Bangalore.

———, 2004, "Capital Formation in Indian Agriculture", *Federation of Farmers Associations: Andhra Pradesh*, Hyderabad.

———, 2004, *Journal of Indian Commerce: January-March*, New Delhi.

———, 2004, "Revisiting the Lending Infrastructure and Changing the Mindset-Critical to Farm Lending", *NABARD News Review: July–December*, Mumbai.

———, 2004, "Revisiting the Lending Infrastructure and Changing the Mindset Critical to Farm Sector", *NABARD News Review: July–December*, Mumbai.

———, 2005, Interview, Business Intelligence Middle East, 5 January, http://www.bi-me.com.

———, 2005, NSS 59th Round, December.

———, 2005, "Preparing the farmers to face the challenges and utilise the opportunities of WTO", *WTO and Its Implications*, New Delhi: Serial Publications.

———, 2006–07, Annual Report, RBI, Mumbai.

———and Reddy, K.C., 2006, "The WTO and South Asian Agriculture, Key Issues and Policy Interventions", *WTO and Implications for South Asia*, K.C. Reddy and T. Nirmala Devi (eds), New Delhi, Serials Publications, 2006, Chapter 3.

———, 2007, "Expert Committee on Agricultural Indebtedness", Mumbai: NABARD.

———, 2008, "Farm loan waivers: The figures don't add up", *The Hindu Business Line*, 4 March.

———, 2008, "Small farmers must get their due share of credit", *The Hindu Business Line*, 13 February.

———, 2010, International trade statistics.

———, 2010, "Rural Land Systems beg for a Change", Liberty Forum Seminar November, www.libertyforum.com.

———, 2010, "Time to break agri-politics nexus", *The Hindu Business Line*, 31 December.

———, 2011, *Inclusion Journal*, Skoch Development Foundation, October–December, pp. 44–46.

———, 2011, Round Table on the Draft Food Security Bill September 2011, PSA, 9 October.

———, 2012, *Inclusion Journal*, January–February, www.skoch.in.

———, 2012, *Inclusion Journal*, January–March, 3(1), pp. 73–75.

———, 2012, Indian Agriculture Report.

———, 2012, "NABARD needs to rethink and reposition", *Inclusion: January –March*, New Delhi.

———, 2013, "Governance in Agriculture", *Inclusion: January–March*, New Delhi: Skoch Development Foundation.

———, 2013, *Inclusion Journal*, January–March.

———, CRAFICARD, RBI.

———, Digital Book: Agricultural Finance – Rural Financial Learning Centre, Kesdees, www.ruralfinance.org.

———, "Land Equity Markets: Shape of the Future", *The Financial Express*.

———, NSS 66th Round.

———, World Development Report, p. 31.

Index